Reprints of Economic Classics

CAPITAL AND POPULATION

CAPITAL

AND

POPULATION

A STUDY OF THE ECONOMIC EFFECTS OF THEIR RELATIONS TO EACH OTHER

BY

FREDERICK B. HAWLEY

[1882]

AUGUSTUS M. KELLEY • PUBLISHERS
CLIFTON 1972

First Edition 1882

(*New York*: D. Appleton & Company, *1, 3 & 5 Bond Street*, 1882)

Reprinted 1972 by

Augustus M. Kelley Publishers

REPRINTS OF ECONOMIC CLASSICS

Clifton New Jersey 07012

Library of Congress Cataloging in Publication Data

Hawley, Frederick Bernard, 1843-1929.
Capital and population.

(Reprints of economic classics)
1. Economics. 2. Mill, John Stuart, 1806-1873.
Principles of political economy. I. Title.
HB171.7.H39 1972 330.1 68-30525
ISBN 0-678-00904-X

PRINTED IN THE UNITED STATES OF AMERICA
by SENTRY PRESS, NEW YORK, N. Y. 10013

CAPITAL

AND

POPULATION:

A STUDY

OF THE

ECONOMIC EFFECTS OF THEIR RELATIONS
TO EACH OTHER.

BY

FREDERICK B. HAWLEY.

NEW YORK:
D. APPLETON AND COMPANY,
1, 3, AND 5 BOND STREET.
1882.

PREFACE.

My position as an economist, as exemplified in this treatise, is a peculiar one. While classing myself, I believe justly, as a strict disciple of what is usually called the English or orthodox school, I have arrived at results, in many instances, diametrically opposed to theirs; especially on the subjects of free trade and taxation. On the other hand, my reasoning presupposes the falsity of most of the arguments heretofore advanced in support of the very conclusions I uphold. As I antagonize the results of one side and the methods of the other, I can look for friends in neither camp. Nevertheless, as the principle I have enunciated really effects the reconciliation of two lines of thought, apparently hopelessly divergent, I may, perhaps, expect to be sustained by those of both sides who prefer construction to destruction.

It would be false modesty in me to seem unaware that the economic law I have attempted to establish equals in its influence upon economic conclusions any hitherto ascertained. Granted its truth, it throws new and decisive light on nearly all the unsolved problems of the science. That it is true, I venture to be the more confident of, because I find it conceded by both Mill and Ricardo, although they failed to apply it, or at all recognize its importance. What I have here attempted is to reason on their lines beyond the limit where they stopped, with the result of greatly modifying and sometimes subverting their conclusions. This I have done without in any case impugning their premises, or controverting their reasoning, further than to show that, while otherwise valid, it was incomplete. My anxiety to place myself in accord with, rather than in antagonism to, these great thinkers has been so great as to lead me to injure the literary form of my work by making it substantially a critique upon Mill's "Principles" instead of an independent and consecutive argument. This has necessitated long quotations, already so familiar to students as to lack interest for them. The importance of showing that my ideas are really but the further development of those of the orthodox school must be my excuse for this; and I shall be pardoned if it has enabled me, as I believe it has, to more readily place the law I enunciate, and in some degree elucidate, in its proper relation to the established truths of the science.

FREDERICK B. HAWLEY.

NEW YORK, *February, 1882.*

CONTENTS.

CAPITAL AND POPULATION.

CHAPTER I.

CAPITAL.

JOHN STUART MILL, in his "Principles of Political Economy," in defining capital, says:

"The distinction, then, between capital and not-capital, does not lie in the kind of commodities, but in the mind of the capitalist—in his will to employ them for one purpose rather than another; and all property, however ill adapted in itself for the use of laborers, is a part of capital, so soon as it, or the value to be received from it, is set apart for productive reinvestment. The sum of all the values so destined by their respective possessors, composes the capital of the country. *Whether all those values are in a shape directly applicable to productive uses, makes no difference. Their shape, whatever it may be, is a temporary accident; but, once destined for production, they do not fail to find a way of transforming themselves into things capable of being applied to it.*"—(Mill, Book I, chapter iv, section 1.)

In Ricardo's works, chapter v, "On Wages," page 51, I find the following definition:

"Capital is that part of the wealth of a country which *is employed in production, and consists of food, clothing, raw materials, machinery, etc., necessary to give effect to labor.*"

It is evident that these definitions differ radically, especially in the passages which I have put in italics.

Mill includes, in the term, all wealth *destined* to productive consumption, whether finally so utilized or not. Until the mental disposition of the holder is changed, it remains capital, and only ceases to be such when its destination is changed to unproductive consumption. He also includes, not only the necessaries and conveniences that will, or may, actually be demanded by the laborer as wages and for the facilities and tools for production, but also the sum of such luxuries as are destined, before being consumed, to be exchanged for such necessaries and conveniences.

Ricardo's meaning is not so clear, on account of the ambiguity of the words "is employed." He seems, however, to intend to confine the term to that part of wealth actually in process of consumption by the laborer for his sustenance, or actually being used by him, as tools or machinery, to facilitate production, and to exclude not only all wealth not fitted for consumption or use by laborers, but such part as is fitted, but not at the time so employed. If this is his meaning, circulating capital becomes identical with what is commonly called "the wages fund," and fixed capital with such part of the machinery, tools, etc., as are actually in use.

It may be, though I do not so understand him, that by "is employed" he means, *is eventually employed*—in which case his definition approaches nearer to that of Mill, but is yet far from being identical with it.

If we attempt to gather his meaning from his writings, we shall find that he uses the term, not only in accordance with both senses of his own definition, though with the first far more often than with the second, but also with the sense in which Mill has defined it. And the same remark will apply to the writings of Mill, who likewise uses it, not only in accordance with his own definition, but in accordance with both senses of Ricardo besides. Mill, indeed, seems utterly oblivious of the fact that his definition differs at all from that of his predecessor; while Ricardo, in passages, exhibits some perception, or rather, perhaps, I should say, an indistinct feeling of the distinction to which I am drawing attention. Among others, I would instance the note to chapter viii, in which he says:

> "There can be no greater error than in supposing that capital is increased by non-consumption. If the price of labor should rise so high that, notwithstanding the increase of capital, no more could be employed, I should say that such increase of capital would be still unproductively consumed."

Ricardo, as we shall see elsewhere,* and as this passage shows, perceived and acknowledged that an increase of capital, in Mill's sense of the term, does not always lead to an increase in his, although his arguments constantly assume that an increase of wealth does practically result in an increase of the wages fund and an increased production. He here perceives the dilemma, and attempts to escape from it by the assertion that such increase of capital is still "unproductively consumed"—i. e., is not capital at all. But in no sense is this true. It is not unproductively consumed in any way or shape, but eventually, though not immediately, productively consumed. He can, if he so chooses to use the word, refuse to call it capital, but he can not claim that it is unproductively consumed, for it is not consumed at all.

* For a further instance, see chapter on wages and profit.

I shall assume throughout this treatise that Ricardo intends to denote, by capital, only such portion of wealth as is actively engaged in production, as it will appear, in the course of the argument, that most of his deductions only hold good when the word is used in this exceedingly restricted sense; and no student of this most exact of deductive reasoners can doubt for a moment his intention of using the term mainly in accordance with the deductions he draws from it. Places can, indeed, be found in his writings where he gives to it a broader signification, and adopts more or less fully its popular use; but when this occurs, the fault must be attributed rather to the application than to the accuracy of his deductions.

The assertion that both Ricardo and Mill used such a fundamental term as capital in various senses, without perceiving that they did so, is a bold one for any one to make, but it has been forced upon me by a careful, and I may say reverential, study of their writings; and I shall, I am sure, be borne out in it by fellow-students when their attention is drawn to the subject. This at least is patent even at this stage of the inquiry, that they defined the term very differently; and it will be acknowledged by all that, starting thus from conflicting definitions, they proceed by the same arguments to identical conclusions. This could hardly have been the case if they had really differed in their understanding of the nature of capital; and I do not fear to assert that in similar parts of their argument they rarely do differ in the sense in which they use the term, notwithstanding the radical difference in their definition of it.

Which definition is correct must be our next consideration; and there can be no doubt but that the preference must be given to that of Mill. We already have a term, viz., the "wages fund," which accurately coincides with "circulating capital" as defined by Ricardo; and a supplementary term can only lead to the further confusion of an intricate subject, while a term to define active fixed capital from idle is not needed. The popular use of the word certainly accords with Mill's definition; and the scientific sense should certainly agree with the popular, in considering as capital all wealth destined to be employed productively, and from which an increase is obtained or hoped for.

Ricardo's definition differs so much from the popular use of the word, that conclusions drawn from it, however correct, are sure to be misunderstood and misapplied in practice. Really valuable results are with difficulty reached, and, when reached, with difficulty appreciated, when the words in which they are expressed are ambiguous. Furthermore, the real object of inquiry is, not how production is effected by the increase of the wages fund —that is a simple matter; but by the general increase of wealth in all its forms—a much more complicated subject.

I would myself prefer a definition of the term, when scientifically used, broader than that of Mill, but not broader than its popular use. Wealth I would define as the existent products of labor, whose utility is not yet exhausted; capital, as that portion of wealth from which an income or profit is expected in addition to a return of the principal. Under this definition national capital would be the same as under Mill's, for no wealth not productively employed can add to the net income of the community, but much wealth not productively employed nevertheless *produces* an income or profit to its possessors. All that part of wealth reserved from immediate for prolonged unproductive consumption, such as houses, places of amusement, works of art, etc., the use and enjoyment of which are a source of income to their possessors, I would prefer to regard as capital to them, though not of course to the community, because to their possessors they are productive. The distinction does not affect this argument, and is of no great importance, further than to notice that such wealth is of no less advantage to the nation than that productively engaged, as, although it adds nothing to the sum of material products, it immediately gratifies desires similar to those ultimately satisfied by material products, and on account of which alone material products have any utility.

Using Mill's or my own definition of capital, it will be necessary to divide it into two portions, which we will call "dead stock" and "active stock": active stock being coincident with that portion of wealth that Ricardo defines as capital, according to our first exemplification of his meaning—i. e., all wealth that is at the time productively engaged; and dead stock being that portion excluded by him and included by Mill—i. e., all wealth destined eventually, but not immediately, to be employed in production.

This distinction is of the first importance, and must be constantly borne in mind during any discussion and investigation of the laws and nature of capital. Although distinctly recognized by all economists,* I know

* Mill, Book I, chapter iv, section 2: "As whatever of the produce of the country is devoted to production is capital, so, conversely, the whole of the capital of the country is devoted to production. This second proposition, however, must be taken with some limitations and explanations. A fund may be seeking for productive employment, and find none adapted to the inclinations of its possessor; it then is capital still, but unemployed capital. Or the stock may consist of unsold goods, not susceptible of direct application to productive uses, and not, at the mo-

of none who have realized its importance, or who have consistently observed it in their arguments. They, one and all, assume that the amount of production depends upon the amount of capital, whereas it is really dependent only on the amount of "active stock," as will be immediately acknowledged by every one who gives the subject a moment's consideration. Ricardo would have been an exception to this criticism, if he had always been consistent with his own definition, faulty as it is. He identified "active stock" and capital; but, if he had fully appreciated the distinction, he could hardly have failed to recognize that he was defining a part of capital as if it were the whole, and that his deductions were not true of the term in its broad sense. More than any other economist, his views coincide with mine, and it is mainly owing to his failure to perceive this distinction that our conclusions differ so radically.

It is as a pupil of his and of Mill that I write, and I wish to be distinctly understood as accepting nearly all the premises and conclusions in both of them not here especially controverted, and to draw attention to the fact that all of my premises, both so far and yet to be advanced, are theirs also with a single exception—the effect

ment, marketable; these, until sold, are in the condition of unemployed capital. Again, artificial or accidental circumstances may render it necessary to possess a larger stock in advance—that is, a larger capital before entering on production—than is required by the nature of things. Suppose that the government lays a tax on the production in one of its earlier stages, as, for instance, by taxing the material. The manufacturer has to advance the tax before commencing the manufacture, and is, therefore, under a necessity of having a larger accumulated fund than is required for, or is actually employed in, the production which he carries on. He must have a larger capital to maintain the same quantity of productive labor."

of a high rate of wages upon population. That my conclusions are in many points different from theirs, is solely due to their neglecting to follow up their own arguments to their proper termination. That they did not do so, we shall see, later on, was due, not so much to the want of logical acumen, as to the fact that there was nothing in their surroundings to suggest further pursuit. The economic condition of England apparently verified their conclusions, and they were naturally satisfied with such verification. I am especially anxious not to be classed in the category of those who have attempted to confute, without understanding, these great writers, but fear I shall not wholly escape, as my conclusions will run counter to some firmly-held opinions, and will conflict with many interests, both national and individual; but I can do no more than proclaim myself their disciple, and disclaim any attempt at refuting the founders of the science. All I shall say is built upon them as a foundation, and all I hope to accomplish is to raise their structure one story higher.

CHAPTER II.

INCREASE OF CAPITAL.

ALL wealth, and therefore all capital, is the result of abstinence. The products of labor may be consumed by the producer, or may be exchanged for other products to be consumed, or such products, whether made by him or acquired, may be reserved for personal consumption; in which cases they are said to be unproductively consumed. If, on the other hand, the producer desires to save what he has brought into being, he can do so in two ways: by employing it as active, or retaining it as dead, stock. He can employ it immediately in sustaining himself and others while engaged in further production, if its nature is fitted for such use; or he can, as soon as possible, exchange it for such things as are so fitted, and then employ them productively; or, if he so elects, he can reserve his product, or the things for which he has exchanged it, to be ultimately but not immediately employed productively by himself or others.

In a barbarous state of society, where each individual endeavors to supply all his wants himself, nearly all produce destined for productive consumption immediately takes the form of "active stock"; * but, when division of

* By the term "active stock" I mean to include not only what is actually at the moment being consumed by the laborer, but also such stock as

labor has been established, some reservation of products must occur, at least sufficient to allow time for exchanges to be effected.

With the exception of the food which farmers reserve for the consumption of themselves, their cattle, and those of their laborers whose wants they immediately supply, very nearly all of the products of civilized labor enter first into "dead stock." All products, which the producer can not himself utilize, necessarily do so.

From this fund of "dead stock" products are distributed to the fund for unproductive consumption and to that for productive consumption. What goes to the former fund, decreases the amount of "dead stock"—what goes to the latter, increases it, as the amount of production is always, on the average, greater than that of the productive consumption which produces it; because, when this ceases to be the case, the motive to produce is taken away. But dead stock may not be distributed at once to either fund, but may be reserved, to await contingencies. Now, what is it that determines the proportion in which the gross stock will be divided between these three funds?

Evidently the relative strength of the desires to accumulate and to enjoy will determine the amount of the fund for unproductive consumption, and the rate of profit the amount of that for productive consumption; but the rate of profit itself depends upon the amount of dead stock. Any increase of dead stock, other things (including gold) remaining the same, lowers its money-value without affecting money-wages; or, if money-wages are lowered, its money-value suffers a yet greater deprecia-

he will require to support him until the product he is engaged upon is completed, and which is preserved by him or for him, for that purpose.

tion.* In the supposed circumstances proportional wages must rise at the expense of profits. But if an increase of dead stock lowers profits, and a decrease of profits discourages the conversion of dead into active stock, it follows that the "wages-fund" will be smallest when dead stock is relatively most abundant, and when the *rate of proportional wages* is the highest. We are entitled, then, to say that the amount of dead stock that will become active depends upon the amount of dead stock itself, and varies inversely with it:

"When the production of a commodity is the effect of labor and expenditure, whether the commodity is susceptible of unlimited multiplication or not, there is a minimum value which is the essential condition of its being permanently produced. The value at any particular time is the result of supply and demand; and is always that which is *necessary to create a market for the existing supply. But unless that value is sufficient to repay the cost of production, and to afford, besides, the ordinary expectation of profit, the commodity will not continue to be produced.* Capitalists will not go on permanently producing at a loss. They will not even go on producing at a profit less than they can live upon. Persons whose capital is already embarked, and can not be easily extricated, will persevere for a considerable time without profit, and have been known to persevere even at a loss, in hope of better times. But they will not do so indefinitely, or when there is nothing to indicate that times are likely to improve. No new capital will be invested in an employ-

* This is not true, of course, when the increase of dead stock consists wholly or largely of money. In such cases prices and profits will rise and proportional wages fall, as happens whenever the currency is inflated. But in all cases, when the increase of dead stock is due wholly to saving, there will be no increase in the amount of money through the operations of exchange until *after* prices have been depressed by such increase of dead stock disturbing the proportion between gold and other commodities. If such increase of stock is universal, the world over, the depression of money prices will be permanent, until such stock is unproductively consumed or the production of gold increased.

ment, unless there be an expectation, not only of some profit, but of a profit as great (regard being had to the degree of eligibility of the employment in other respects) as can be hoped for in any other occupation at that time and place. When such profit is evidently not to be had, if people do not actually withdraw their capital, they at least abstain from replacing it when consumed. The cost of production, together with the ordinary profit, may, therefore, be called the *necessary* price or value of all things made by labor and capital. Nobody willingly produces in the prospect of loss. Whoever does so, does it under a miscalculation, which he corrects as fast as he is able."—(Mill, Book III, chapter iii, section 1.)

We have supposed in the above argument that "other things remained the same." What was included under that head was the state of the arts, social customs and regulations, the natural fertility of the soil, and the number of the population. Improvement in the two former conditions, or any increase in the two latter, will of course allow of a corresponding increase of dead stock, without its being followed by a rise of proportional wages and fall in profits; and such increase will go partly to swell the wages-fund or active stock. It is only when the increase of capital outstrips the others that a diminution of the wages-fund and a rise of wages will occur. Economists have, I believe universally, held that such diminution of the wages-fund could be but temporary; because the stimulus to population of a high *rate* of wages would, before very long, readjust the ratio between capital and population. But the real stimulus to population is not a high *rate* of wages in the sense in which wages are compared with profits, because that surely entails a lessening of employment, but a low rate, because then nearly all the members of the laboring class are earning something, and the average of the necessities and comforts of life that laborers, employed and unemployed, receive is then greater than when some are receiving high wages and many are receiving none at all. In other words, the stimulus to population is affected not by the rate of proportional wages, as economists have hithero universally assumed, but by the proportion between the gross amount of the wages-fund and the number of those depending upon it for subsistence—a very different thing, for such proportion is always the least when the rate of proportional wages is highest.

The normal ratio between capital and population, when disturbed by an increase of capital, can not therefore be restored by the stimulus to population afforded by such increase; because its tendency is not to stimulate, but to restrain. The proper proportion of dead stock can only be restored, in the absence of exceptional circumstances, by an increase of unproductive consumption, which directly decreases the fund, or by converting less of it into active stock, which indirectly decreases the fund, by preventing further additions to it being made, and thus allows the ordinary, or even a less than ordinary, unproductive consumption to deplete it. But the former of these causes can not, or rather will not, act, because, when an excess of dead stock lessens both profits and the wages-fund, neither capitalists nor laborers will have as large incomes to expend, and they will consequently consume less unproductively than before, instead of more, and will thus retard instead of assist the readjustment.

An excess of dead stock can only be practically done away with by decreasing production, and the only way to escape the necessity of so doing is to prevent a growth of capital faster than that of population.

The reader will please notice that I do not here assert over-production to be an evil, but only that over-accumulation leads necessarily to a lessened production, and that such lessened production is an evil.

The importance of the preceding paragraphs to the argument can hardly be overstated, and I emphasize them by thus drawing attention to them, fearing from the brevity of my statement that the importance of the principles involved will not be enough considered. They are the only necessary premises that I use, for which I am unable to find any authority in Mill and Ricardo themselves. Their truth can not be doubted, nor can it be gainsaid that, if Mill and Ricardo had taken notice of the fact that increase of dead stock decreases active stock, and restrains population instead of stimulating it, they would have modified their conclusions very nearly, if not quite, in accordance with mine.

I now desire to verify, by quotation and criticism, the somewhat bold charge I have made in the preceding chapter, that both these writers use the fundamental term "capital" loosely and inaccurately, and in conflicting senses.

In Book II, chapter xi, section 3, Mill says:

"Wages depend, then, on the proportion between the number of the laboring population and the capital, or other funds, devoted to the purchase of labor; we will say, for shortness, the capital. If wages are higher at one time or place than at another, if the subsistence and comfort of the class of hired laborers are more ample, it is for no other reason than because capital bears a greater proportion to population. It is not the absolute amount of accumulation or of production that is of importance to the laboring class; it is not the amount even of the funds destined for distribution among the laborers; it is the proportion between those funds and the numbers among whom they are shared. The condition of the class can be bettered in no other way than by altering that proportion to their advantage; and every scheme for their benefit, which does not proceed on this as its foundation, is, for all permanent purposes, a delusion."

This passage singularly exemplifies Mill's confusion of thought on the subject we are discussing. In his first sentence, if he means by wages real wages, they depend mainly on the margin of cultivation, and, in so far as they are affected by it, do not depend directly but inversely on the amount of capital, as he defines it; though they do depend upon it in Ricardo's sense of the term. If by wages he means proportional wages, they depend not upon "the number of the laboring population," but upon the ratio of the value of the wages-fund to the value of the product. In his second sentence he treats the two clauses, "if wages are higher at one time or place than at another" and "if the subsistence and comfort of the class of hired laborers are more ample," as identical propositions. If he means by wages the rate of real wages—i. e., the average sum of necessaries and comforts each laborer employed or unemployed receives—they are identical; but neither assertion is true, unless he uses capital in the sense of Ricardo; and it is hardly supposable that he does so use it, as it is very unlikely that he should attach the importance he seems to, to so simple a statement as that, the amount each laborer receives can be found by dividing the wages-fund by the number of laborers, and yet that is all the statement will then include. If he means proportional wages, and adheres to his own definition of capital, they are not identical, as his proposition is true as to the first clause and not true as to the second. If he uses the term in Ricardo's sense, they are likewise not identical, as the second is true and the first not. Whichever way we interpret Mill's meaning, we find an inaccuracy or an inconsistency.

Now let us compare Mill's account of the possible increase of capital with that I have ventured to present.

In Book I, chapter v, section 3, he says:

" While, on the one hand, industry is limited by capital, so, on the other, every increase of capital gives, or is capable of giving, additional employment to industry; and this without assignable limit. I do not mean to deny that the capital, or part of it, may be so employed as not to support laborers, being fixed in machinery, buildings, improvement of land, and the like. In any large increase of capital a considerable portion will generally be thus employed, and will only co-operate with laborers, not maintain them. What I do intend to assert is, that the portion which is *destined* to their maintenance may (supposing no alteration in anything else) be indefinitely increased, without creating an impossibility of finding them employment; in other words, that if there are human beings capable of work, and food to feed them, they may always be employed in producing something. This proposition requires to be somewhat dwelt upon, being one of those which it is exceedingly easy to assent to when presented in general terms, but somewhat difficult to keep fast hold of in the crowd and confusion of the actual facts of society. It is also very much opposed to common doctrines. There is not an opinion more general among mankind than this, that the unproductive expenditure of the rich is necessary to the employment of the poor. Before Adam Smith, the doctrine had hardly been questioned; and ever since his time, authors of the highest name and of great merit* have contended that if consumers were to save and convert into capital more than a limited portion of their income, and were not to devote to unproductive consumption an amount of means bearing a certain ratio to the capital of the country, the extra accumulation would be merely so much waste, since there would be no market for the commodities which the capital so created would produce. I conceive this to be one of the many errors arising in political economy, from the practice of not beginning with the examination of simple cases, but rushing at once into the complexity of concrete phenomena. Every one can see that if a benevolent government possessed all the food, and all the implements and materials, of the community, it could exact productive labor from all capable of it, to whom it allowed a share in the food, and could be in no danger of wanting a field for the em-

* For example, Mr. Malthus, Dr. Chalmers, M. de Sismondi.

ployment of this productive labor, since as long as there was a single want unsaturated (which material objects could supply) of any one individual, the labor of the community could be turned to the production of something capable of satisfying that want. Now, the individual possessors of capital, when they add to it by fresh accumulations, are doing precisely the same thing which we suppose to be done by a benevolent government. As it is allowable to put any case by way of hypothesis, let us imagine the most extreme case conceivable. Suppose that every capitalist came to be of opinion that, not being more meritorious than a well-conducted laborer, he ought not to fare better; and accordingly laid by, from conscientious motives, the surplus of his profits; or suppose this abstinence not spontaneous, but imposed by law or opinion upon all capitalists, and upon land-owners likewise. Unproductive expenditure is now reduced to its lowest limit; and it is asked, How is the increased capital to find employment? Who is to buy the goods which it will produce? There are no longer customers even for those which were produced before. The goods, therefore (it is said), will remain unsold; they will perish in the warehouses, until capital is brought down to what it was originally, or rather to as much less, as the demand of the consumers has lessened. But this is seeing only one half of the matter. In the case supposed, there would no longer be any demand for luxuries, on the part of capitalists and land-owners. But when these classes turn their income into capital, they do not thereby annihilate their power of consumption; they do but transfer it from themselves to the laborers to whom they give employment. Now, there are two possible suppositions in regard to the laborers; either there is, or there is not, an increase of their numbers, proportional to the increase of capital. If there is, the case offers no difficulty. The production of necessaries for the new population takes the place of the production of luxuries for a portion of the old, and supplies exactly the amount of employment which has been lost. But suppose that there is no increase of population. The whole of what was previously expended in luxuries, by capitalists and landlords, is distributed among the existing laborers, in the form of additional wages. We will assume them to be already sufficiently supplied with necessaries. What follows? That the laborers become consumers of luxuries, and the capital previously employed in the production of luxuries is still able to employ itself in the same manner; the difference being, that the luxuries are shared among the community generally, instead of being confined to a few. The increased accumulation and increased production might, rigorously speaking, continue, until every laborer had every indulgence of wealth, consistent with continuing to work; supposing that the power of their labor were physically sufficient to produce all this amount of indulgences for their whole number. Thus the limit of wealth is never deficiency of consumers, but of producers and productive power. Every addition to capital gives to labor either additional employment, or additional remuneration; enriches either the country or the laboring class. If it finds additional hands to set to work, it increases the aggregate produce; if only the same hands, it gives them a larger share of it; and perhaps even in this case, by stimulating them to greater exertions, augments the produce itself."

Even if we assent to every subsequent proposition in this quotation, the assertion in the first sentence, that "every increase of capital gives or is capable of giving additional employment to industry, and this without assignable limit," is not true. If we suppose population to keep pace with or increase faster than capital, the time must eventually arrive when every capitalist and laborer is reduced to the barest necessities; and then a further increase of capital can not lead to any increase in population or production. Such further increase, which must come entirely from rentals, would then surely fail to give "additional employment or remuneration to industry." If population did not increase as fast as capital, the time would eventually arrive when all the population in existence, willing to work for all they produced, would be employed in the most advantageous manner that the state of the arts would allow. An increase of capital, then, coming from rent or wages (it could not come from profits, as they would be annihilated), could give no additional employment, for there would be no more laborers to be set to work. There are then "assignable limits" to capital, even under the wildest and most improbable suppositions.

But, passing this, if we hold Mill to his definition, the whole reasoning is unsound, for the infinite increase of capital he supposes might go to the increase of dead and not of active stock, as indeed it would, capitalists being human; in which case no more labor would be employed than before it took place. If, on the other hand, by capital he means the wages-fund, his argument is true enough, but more curious than valuable. Indeed, I fail to see how it can in any sense be called political economy. I have always conceived that science to be an inquiry into the acquisition and distribution of wealth, not by disinterestedly benevolent beings, but by self-interested men. That men will act in accordance with their real or supposed interest, is the major premise of all economic reasoning. I do not know to what science to refer an argument based on the supposition that any class of men will not do so, but I am quite certain that such science is not economic. This whole quotation is an attempt to show what would, or could, occur if capitalists were content to go on producing with no hope of a gain. Is there a single economic doctrine that can stand such a test? What would become of Malthus's theory of population, if laborers would work without wages? What of Ricardo's theory of rent, if landlords and tenants were indifferent to the rentals paid and received? What of the proposition that profits tended to equalization, if capitalists were careless of what profit they obtained? And yet we are asked to believe that over-accumulation is impossible, because it would be so if capitalists were indifferent to profit, and we are scouted as ignorant visionaries if we venture to suggest that it may be the cause of our periods of industrial stagnation. Mill says:

> "Authors, of the highest name and of great merit, have contended that if consumers were to save and convert into capital more than a limited portion of their income, and were not to devote to unproductive consumption an amount of means bearing a certain ratio to the capital of the country, the extra accumulation would be merely so much waste, since there would be no *market* for the commodities which the capital, so created, would produce."

If he merely means to assert, following Say, that the supply of commodities constitutes the demand, what he says is true, but is inapplicable to the discussion. The word "market," as used by his opponents, implies very much more than he seems to suppose, and the sense in which they use the word is its proper signification, both popularly and scientifically. When men speak of a good or bad market, they do not mean a market in which more goods can be bought than can be sold, or *vice versa*, but they mean a market in which, at the going prices, goods can be exchanged for such amount of money or other things as will, when expended in production, more than reproduce or less than reproduce the original things. If the goods will buy more labor than it took to produce them, the market is good; if less, the market is poor. Now insert before the word "market" the word "remunerative," and, tautological though it be, the addition makes it evident that Mill's opponents have given a true and valid reason for all their assertions.

I do not remember to have anywhere seen the observation that Say's principle, applied as Mill applies it, proves as well that no single commodity can be in excess, as that material commodities generally can not be so. No matter what the quantity of a single commodity, it would exchange for something; and we can not say of it that more has been produced than *can be exchanged*, and likewise we can not say this of commodities generally, but we can say both of single commodities and material commodities in general, that more has been produced than *will be exchanged;* and this is all that there is any necessity of affirming to establish the fact that over-accumulation and general glut can occur. In the sense of our discussion, labor is a commodity, though not a material one. When the possibility of a general glut is asserted, it is not meant that both labor and material commodities may be in excess, but only that all material things may be in excess as compared with labor—the one great immaterial commodity. In that sense, and it is the sense in which its advocates have really used the term, a more or less general glut is not only a possible but a frequent occurrence.

As this is an important point in the discussion, I make another quotation from Mill—premising that a "general glut" is the result of over-accumulation and not of over-production. Excessive production, supposing such a thing possible, need not necessarily result in accumulation at all. To affirm that over-production and over-accumulation are equivalent things, can only be done on the supposition that Mill's definition of capital coincides with Ricardo's; or, in other words, that all wealth destined for productive consumption immediately constitutes the wages-fund.

Accumulation will ordinarily be large when the production is great, because production will not be great unless profits are high, and savings are mainly made from profits; but there is no necessary connection between them, as many things can intervene to prevent accumulation in such times. There is, of course, a tendency for rapid production to result in excessive accumulation; and it is the counteraction of this tendency that Mill argues against and that I advocate.

To fully present Mill's reasoning to the reader, I here quote at great length from Book III, chapter xiv, section 1:

"After the elementary exposition of the theory of money contained in the last few chapters, we shall return to a question in the general theory of value, which could not be satisfactorily discussed until the nature and operations of money were in some measure understood, because the errors, against which we have to contend, mainly originate in a misunderstanding of these operations.

"We have seen that the value of everything gravitates toward a certain medium point (which has been called the natural value), namely, that at which it exchanges for every other thing in the ratio of their cost of production. We have seen, too, that the actual or market value coincides, or nearly so, with the natural value only on an average of years, and is continually either rising above or falling below it, from alterations in the demand, or casual fluctuations in the supply; but that these variations correct themselves, through the tendency of the supply to accommodate itself to the demand which exists for the commodity at its natural value. A general convergence thus results from the balance of opposite divergences. Dearth, or scarcity, on the one hand, and over-supply, or, in mercantile language, glut, on the other, are incident to all commodities. In the first case the commodity affords to the producers or sellers, while the deficiency lasts, an unusually high rate of profit; in the second, the supply being in excess of that for which a demand exists, at such a value as will afford the ordinary profit, the sellers must be content with less, and must, in extreme cases, submit to a loss.

"Because this phenomenon of over-supply, and consequent inconvenience or loss to the producer or dealer, may exist in the case of any one commodity whatever, many persons, including some distinguished political economists, have thought that it may exist with regard to all commodities; that there may be a general over-production of wealth; a supply of commodities in the aggregate, surpassing the demand; and a consequent depressed condition of all classes of producers. Against this doctrine, of which Mr. Malthus and Dr. Chalmers in this country, and M. de Sismondi on the Continent, were the chief apostles, I have already contended in the First Book; * but it was not possible, in that stage of our inquiry, to enter into a complete examination of an error (as I conceive) essentially grounded on a misunderstanding of the phenomena of value and price.

"The doctrine appears to me to involve so much inconsistency in its very conception, that I feel considerable difficulty in giving any statement of it which shall be at once clear, and satisfactory to its supporters. They agree in maintaining that there may be, and sometimes is, an excess of productions in general beyond the demand for them; that when this happens, purchasers can not be found at prices which will repay the cost of production with a profit; that there ensues a general depression of prices or values (they are seldom accurate in discriminating between the two), so that producers, the more they produce, find themselves the poorer, instead of richer; and Dr Chalmers accordingly inculcates on capitalists the practice of a moral restraint in reference to the pursuit of gain; while Sismondi deprecates machinery, and the various inventions which increase productive power. They both maintain that accumulation of capital may proceed too fast, not merely for the moral but for the material interests of those who produce and accumulate; and they enjoin the rich to guard against this evil by an ample unproductive consumption.

"When these writers speak of the supply of commodities as outrunning the demand, it is not clear which of the two elements of demand they have in view—the desire to possess, or the means of purchase; whether their meaning is that there are, in such cases, more consumable products in existence than the public desires to consume, or merely more than it is able to pay for. In this uncertainty, it is necessary to examine both suppositions.

"First, let us suppose that the quantity of commodities produced is not greater than the community would be glad to consume; is it, in that case, possible that there should be a deficiency of demand

* *Supra*, pp. 41–43.

for all commodities, for want of the means of payment? Those who think so, can not have considered what it is which constitutes the means of payment for commodities. It is, simply, commodities Each person's means of paying for the productions of other people consists of those which he himself possesses. All sellers are inevitably, and by the meaning of the word, buyers. Could we suddenly double the productive powers of the country, we should double the supply of commodities in every market; but we should, by the same stroke, double the purchasing power. Everybody would bring a double demand as well as supply; everybody would be able to buy twice as much, because every one would have twice as much to offer in exchange. It is probable, indeed, that there would now be a superfluity of certain things. Although the community would willingly double its aggregate consumption, it may already have as much as it desires of some commodities, and it may prefer to do more than double its consumption of others, or to exercise its increased purchasing power on some new thing. If so, the supply will adapt itself accordingly, and the values of things will continue to conform to their cost of production. At any rate, it is a sheer absurdity that all things should fall in value, and that all producers should, in consequence, be insufficiently remunerated. If values remain the same, what becomes of prices is immaterial, since the remuneration of producers does not depend on how much money but on how much of consumable articles they obtain for their goods. Besides, money is a commodity; and if all commodities are supposed to be doubled in quantity, we must suppose money to be doubled too, and then prices would no more fall than values would.

"A general over-supply, or excess of all commodities above the demand, so far as demand consists in means of payment, is thus shown to be an impossibility. But it may, perhaps, be supposed that it is not the ability to purchase, but the desire to possess, that falls short, and that the general produce of industry may be greater than the community desires to consume—the part, at least, of the community which has an equivalent to give. It is evident enough that produce makes a market for produce, and that there is wealth in the country with which to purchase all the wealth in the country; but those who have the means may not have the wants, and those who have the wants may be without the means. A portion, therefore, of the commodities produced may be unable to find a market, from the absence of means in those who have the desire to consume, and the want of desire in those who have the means.

"This is much the most plausible form of the doctrine, and does not, like that which we first examined, involve a contradiction. There may easily be a greater quantity of any particular commodity than is desired by those who have the ability to purchase, and it is abstractedly conceivable that this might be the case with all commodities. The error is in not perceiving that, though all who have an equivalent to give might be fully provided with every consumable article which they desire, the fact that they go on adding to the production proves that this is not actually the case. Assume the most favorable hypothesis for the purpose, that of a limited community, every member of which possesses as much of necessaries and of all known luxuries as he desires; and since it is not conceivable that persons whose wants were completely satisfied would labor and economize to obtain what they did not desire, suppose that a foreigner arrives, and produces an additional quantity of something of which there was already enough. Here, it will be said, is over-production; true, I reply; over-production of that particular article: the community wanted no more of that, but it wanted something. The old inhabitants, indeed, wanted nothing; but did not the foreigner himself want something? When he produced the superfluous article, was he laboring without a motive? He has produced, but the wrong thing instead of the right. He wanted, perhaps, food, and has produced watches, with which everybody was sufficiently supplied. The new-comer brought with him into the country a demand for commodities equal to all that he could produce by his industry, and it was his business to see that the supply he brought should be suitable to that demand. If he could not produce something capable of exciting a new want or desire in the community, for the satisfaction of which some one would grow more food and give it to him in exchange, he had the alternative of growing food for himself; either on fresh land, if there was any unoccupied, or as a tenant, or partner, or servant, of some former occupier, willing to be partially relieved from labor. He has produced a thing not wanted, instead of what was wanted; and he himself, perhaps, is not the kind of producer who is wanted; but there is no over-production: production is not excessive but merely ill-assorted. We saw before that whoever brings additional commodities to the market, brings an additional power of purchase; we now see that he brings also an additional desire to consume; since, if he had not that desire, he would not have troubled himself to produce. Neither of the elements of demand, therefore, can be wanting when there is an additional supply; though it is perfectly possible that the demand may be for one thing, and the supply may unfortunately consist of another.

"Driven to his last retreat, an opponent may perhaps allege that there are persons who produce and accumulate from mere habit; not because they have any object in growing richer, or desire to add in any respect to their consumption, but from *vis inertiæ*. They continue producing because the machine is ready mounted, and save and reinvest their savings because they have nothing on which they care to expend them. I grant that this is possible, and in some few instances probably happens; but these do not in the smallest degree affect our conclusion. For, what do these persons do with their savings? They invest them productively;* that is, expend them in employing labor. In other words, having a purchasing power belonging to them, more than they know what to do with, they make over the surplus of it for the general benefit of the laboring class. Now, will that class also not know what to do with it? Are we to suppose that they too have their wants perfectly satisfied, and go on laboring from mere habit? Until this is the case; until the working classes have also reached the point of satiety—there will be no want of demand for the produce of capital, however rapidly it may accumulate; since, if there is nothing else for it to do, it can always find employment in producing the necessaries or luxuries of the laboring class. And when they too had no further desire for necessaries or luxuries, they would take the benefit of any further increase of wages by diminishing their work; so that the over-production, which then for the first time would be possible in idea could not even then take place in fact, for want of laborers. Thus, in whatever manner the question is looked at, even though we go to the extreme verge of possibility to invent a supposition favorable to it, the theory of general over-production implies an absurdity.

* That is just what they do not do—they add them to dead stock, and keep them inactive until the rate of profit tempts them to employ them productively.

"What, then, is it by which men who have reflected much on economical phenomena, and have even contributed to throw new light upon them by original speculations, have been led to embrace so irrational a doctrine? I conceive them to have been deceived by a mistaken interpretation of certain mercantile facts. They imagined that the possibility of a general over-supply of commodities was proved by experience. They believed that they saw this phenomenon in certain conditions of the markets, the true explanation of which is totally different.

"I have already described the state of the markets for commodities which accompanies what is termed a commercial crisis. At such times there is really an excess of all commodities above the money-demand; in other words, there is an under-supply of money. From the sudden annihilation of a great mass of credit, every one dislikes to part with ready money, and many are anxious to procure it at any sacrifice. Almost everybody, therefore, is a seller, and there are scarcely any buyers: so that there may really be, though only while the crisis lasts, an extreme depression of general prices from what may be indiscriminately called a glut of commodities or a dearth of money. But it is a great error to suppose, with Sismondi, that a commercial crisis is the effect of a general excess of production. It is simply the consequence of an excess of speculative purchases. It is not a gradual advent of low prices, but a sudden recoil from prices extravagantly high: its immediate cause is a contraction of credit, and the remedy is not a diminution of supply, but the restoration of confidence. It is also evident that this temporary derangement of markets is an evil only because it is temporary. The fall being solely of money-prices, if prices did not rise again no dealer would lose, since the smaller price would be worth as much to him as the larger price was before. In no manner does this phenomenon answer to the description which these celebrated economists have given of the evil of over-production. That permanent decline in the circumstances of producers, for want of markets, which those writers contemplate, is a conception to which the nature of a commercial crisis gives no support.

"The other phenomenon from which the notion of a general excess of wealth and superfluity of accumulation seems to derive countenance, is one of a more permanent nature, namely, the fall of profits and interest which naturally takes place with the progress of population and production. The cause of this decline of profit is the increased cost of maintaining labor, which results from an increase of population and of the demand for food outstripping the advance of agricultural improvement. This important feature in the economical progress of nations will receive full consideration and discussion in the succeeding book. It is obviously a totally different thing from a want of market for commodities, though often confounded with it in the complaints of the producing and trading classes. *The true interpretation of the modern or present state of industrial economy is, that there is hardly any amount of business which may not be done if people will be content to do it on small profits;* and this all active and intelligent persons in business perfectly well know: but even those who comply with the necessities of their time, grumble at what they comply with, and wish that there were less capital; or, as they express it, less competition, in order that there might be greater profits. Low profits, however, are a different thing from deficiency of demand, and the production and accumulations, which merely reduce profits, can not be called excess of supply or production. What the phenomenon really is, and its effects and necessary limits, will be seen when we treat of that express subject.

"I know not of any economical facts, except the two I have specified, which can have given occasion to the opinion that a general over-production of commodities ever presented itself in actual experience. I am convinced that there is no fact in commercial affairs which, in order to its explanation, stands in need of that chimerical supposition.

"The point is fundamental; any difference of opinion on it involves radically different conceptions of political economy, especially in its practical aspect. On the one view, we have only to consider how a sufficient production may be combined with the best possible distribution; but, on the other, there is a third thing to be considered: how a market can be created for produce, or how production can be limited to the capabilities of the market. Besides, a theory so essentially self-contradictory can not intrude itself without carrying confusion into the very heart of the subject, and making it impossible even to conceive with any distinctness many of the more complicated economical workings of society. This error has been, I conceive, fatal to the systems, as systems, of the three distinguished economists to whom I have referred—Malthus, Chalmers, and Sismondi—all of whom have admirably conceived and explained several of the elementary theorems of political economy; but this fatal misconception has spread itself, like a veil, between them and the more difficult portions of the subject, not suffering one ray of light to penetrate. Still more is this same confused idea constantly crossing and bewildering the speculations of minds inferior to theirs. It is but justice to two eminent names, to call attention to the fact that the merit of having placed this most important point in its true light belongs principally, on the Continent, to the judicious J. B. Say, and in this country to Mr. Mill, who (besides the conclusive exposition which he gave of the subject in his 'Elements of Political Economy') had set forth the correct doctrine with great force and clearness in an early pamphlet, called forth by a temporary controversy, and entitled 'Commerce Defended'; the first of his writings which attained any celebrity, and which he prized more as having been his first introduction to the friendship of David Ricardo, the most valued and most intimate friendship of his life."

It is, of course, needless to point out that here again Mill uses capital in the sense of Ricardo. It will also be noticed that over-accumulation and over-production are not at all distinguished, and that arguments valid against the latter are taken for granted as valid against the former also.

As to the argument, it is, of course, true when *money* and *labor* are considered as commodities; but what the advocates of over-accumulation assert, and what Mill is really interested in denying, is only that the amount of all *material* commodities can be and sometimes is excessive. That this is what Mill opposes is evident from section 4, in which he refuses to accept over-accumulation as an explanation of panics. It would be too absurd to suppose that any one claimed that panics were due to an excess of labor as well as of material commodities; and, therefore, Mill's meaning must be that the excess of material commodities has no influence in leading to industrial stagnation. This is the objective point of his whole argument, and all his disciples, notably Bonamy Price and Fawcett, have so understood and accepted him, and in the most unequivocal terms have attributed the lessened production of such periods to the general poverty resulting from the extravagance of preceding periods of high profits and large production.

Now, it is evident that the whole argument, contained in the quotation I have last made, is inapplicable to the conclusion thus drawn. Fortunately, there is a test which can not but be accepted, as decisive between the view of Mill's disciples and my own, by any who doubt. To this test I am anxious to draw the closest attention, as no one who appreciates its significance can, I think, fail to agree with me. *If any particular panic and the period of industrial idleness which follows it are caused by the poverty of the community—i. e., by the amount of material commodities being less than usual—the rate of profit during such panic and period will be high (not the rate of interest, which is then liable to violent fluctuations and does not at all indicate the rate of profit); for what capital is left in the community can not fail of finding profitable employment. If, on the contrary, the rate of profit is low, it can be due to no other cause than that capital bears a larger proportion than usual to population.*

In Book II, chapter viii, section 3, Mill, speaking of prices, says:

"It is to be remarked that this ratio would be precisely that in which the quantity of money had been increased. If the whole money in circulation was doubled, prices would be doubled. If it was only increased one fourth, prices would rise one fourth. There would be one fourth more money, all of which would be used to purchase goods of some description. When there had been time for the increased supply of money to reach all markets, or (according to the conventional metaphor) to permeate all the channels of circulation, all prices would have risen one fourth. But the general rise of prices is independent of this diffusing and equalizing process. Even if some prices were raised more, and others less, the average rise would be one fourth. This is a necessary consequence of the fact that a fourth more money would have been given for only the same quantity of goods. *General* prices, therefore, would in any case be a fourth higher.

"The very same effect would be produced on prices if we suppose the goods diminished, instead of the money increased; and the contrary effect if the goods were increased, or the money diminished. If there were less money in the hands of the community, and the same amount of goods to be sold, less money altogether would be given for them, and they would be sold at lower prices; lower, too, in the precise ratio in which the money was diminished. So that the value of money, other things being the same, varies inversely as its quantity; every increase of quantity lowering the value, and every diminution raising it, in a ratio exactly equivalent.

"This, it must be observed, is a property peculiar to money. We did not find it to be true of commodities generally that every diminution of supply raised the value exactly in proportion to the deficiency, or that every increase lowered it in the precise ratio of the excess. Some things are usually affected in a greater ratio than that of the excess of deficiency, others usually in a less; because, in ordinary cases of demand, the desire, being for the thing itself, may be stronger or weaker; and the amount of what people are willing to expend on it, being in any case a limited quantity, may be affected in very unequal degrees by difficulty or facility of attainment. But in the case of money, which is desired as the means of universal purchase, the demand consists of everything which people have to sell; and the only limit to what they are willing to give, is the limit set by their having nothing more to offer. The whole of the goods being in any case exchanged for the whole of the money which comes into the market to be laid out, they will sell for less or more of it, exactly according as less or more is bought.

"From what precedes, it might for a moment be supposed that

all the goods on sale in a country at any one time, are exchanged for all the money existing and in circulation at that same time; or, in other words, that there is always in circulation in a country a quantity of money equal in value to the whole of the goods then and there on sale. But this would be a complete misapprehension. The money laid out is equal in value to the goods it purchases; but the quantity of money laid out is not the same thing with the quantity in circulation. As the money passes from hand to hand, the same piece of money is laid out many times, before all the things on sale at one time are purchased and finally removed from the market; and each pound or dollar must be counted for as many pounds or dollars as the number of times it changes hands, in order to effect this object."

This passage supplies another test of whether any particular period of activity or stagnation is due to a large or small amount of disposable wealth. If, for instance, low prices generally prevail during a period of inactivity, it shows that the stock of commodities must be large as compared with the stock of money. If the industrial inactivity is due to a scarcity of circulating capital, using the term according to Mill's definition, prices should be high, unless there has been an enormous exportation of gold; but the movement of gold—except when driven out by an irredeemable currency, which then becomes money, and, as far as prices are affected, supplies its function—is always too insignificant to account for the variations in general prices which occur, as will be evident when we reflect that the rise or fall must always be mathematically proportional; that is, if the stock of commodities remains the same, one quarter of the gold of the country must be exported to account for a fall in general prices of twenty-five per cent, and, if the stock of commodities has also diminished, it would only account for a fall proportionally less by the percentage of such diminution. We are forced, therefore, to account for such falls in general prices by supposing that they are due to an actual increase of material commodities. As prices are always low during hard, and high during flush times, it necessarily follows that it is during the former that the amount of material wealth is greatest.

We see, therefore, that low prices prevailing during any period of stagnation are an indication that the depression is not caused by poverty, but by excessive accumulations; but they are not as good a test as that of low profits. If any improvement be made, such, for instance, as the establishment of a clearing-house, other things remaining the same, a certain amount of gold is not needed and must be exported. This can only be effected through a rise in prices. Rapidity of circulation tends to raise prices, and sluggishness to depress them. During good times, therefore, the greater efficiency of money tends to raise prices beyond the point they would otherwise attain, and during bad times its greater sluggishness correspondingly depresses them. This produces the same effect upon prices as the proportion between money and other commodities, and low prices are not, therefore, as accurate a test as low profits of the true cause of the industrial inactivity, but they possess the advantage of being more readily ascertained and compared.

Mill admits that any one commodity may be in excess. He must therefore also grant that all but one can be so. If that one exception is labor, his opponents have granted to them all they claim and he denies. Mill truly says:

"The point is fundamental; any difference of opinion on it involves radically different conceptions of political economy, especially in its practical aspect."

But he is at sea when he goes on to assert:

> "On the one view, we have only to consider how a sufficient production may be combined with the best possible distribution; but, on the other, there is a third thing to be considered—how a market can be created for produce, or how a production can be limited to the capabilities of the market."

The practical application of the theory of over-accumulation involves no such considerations as he here supposes. It indeed concerns itself with limiting the tendency to accumulate, but it effects by this a greater not a lessened production, and all it does to secure a "market" is to endeavor to sustain a rate of profit under which production can go on most readily.

As to Say's famous argument, with which I am in entire accord, it is enough to call attention to the fact that, though commodities, no matter how great their quantity, will exchange for each other freely, if they are produced in such proportions as to satisfy the desires of those who exert an efficient demand, such proportions are *ipso facto* not sustained when a certain and natural proportion between the demand for productive and for unproductive consumption is not maintained. My whole position is granted by Mill when he says, "The true interpretation of the modern or present state of industrial economy is, that there is hardly any amount of business which may not be done, if people will be content to do it on small profits." Very well, then. Let us attribute our periods of industrial inactivity to low profits. *Nothing is more certain than that people will cease producing as profits decline, and that they must so decline when capital increases faster than population.*

I complain of Mill, not only that he is confused in his theoretical conceptions as to capital and accumulation, but that he entirely failed to appreciate their practical bearing upon production, as is evidenced by his attempt to explain panics as due alone to the action of credit, and by his constant exhortations to abstinence.

Let us now turn to Ricardo, who, in his chapter on "Taxes on Raw Produce," page 95, says:

"An accumulation of capital naturally produces an increased competition among the employers of labor, and a consequent rise in its price."

If in this sentence he uses the term "capital" according to his own definition, he is not entitled to use the term "accumulation of capital" at all, as applied to circulating capital, which alone affects the competition for labor. Capital, according to him, being merely the wages-fund, does not become capital until it is expended, and is physically incapable of being accumulated; or, if we suppose him to include under capital funds set apart for the maintenance of the laborer until the product he is then engaged upon is brought to market, there can be no increase of the wages-fund beyond that amount. Anything set apart for the employment of labor, beyond that at the time employed, is not capital in his sense, but in Mill's. But it is only such increase of capital that can affect the competition for labor. The demand for and supply of labor do not at all depend upon capital, in his sense of the term. The wages-fund is the effect and not the cause of the demand for labor. The word, therefore, must be used in the sense in which Mill defines the term, and in that sense his assertion is inaccurate.

Population being stationary, an increase of capital beyond the limits I have pointed out decreases the demand for labor. The demand for labor must, then, depend upon something else. The proportion that determines the demand is not between commodities already in existence and the number of laborers, but between the commodities needed, or supposed to be needed, sufficiently to sell for a profit, and the number of laborers. It is not between the accumulations of past production and labor, but between the amount of future production and labor. But the amount of future production supposed to be needed will be least when things already in existence are most plenty, and greatest when they are scarce, and the direct opposite of Ricardo's assertion as to the demand for labor is what really follows. As to its price, he is right if he means relative price, but not otherwise.

As a rule, Ricardo is more faithful to his definition than Mill is to his. Accepting his faulty definition, his conclusions are accurately true. Mill, on the other hand, persistently asserts Ricardo's conclusions as also true of capital as he defines it, and is, therefore, much more at fault than his predecessor. Sometimes, however, as in our quotation, Ricardo himself applies conclusions only true of the wages-fund to capital in its broader and truer signification.

Although not strictly in the line of our argument, it may be well here to notice the principle enunciated by Mill, that the demand for commodities is not a demand for labor, as it is connected with our subject, and its consideration will throw additional light on the discussion. This proposition has attained the place of the *pons asinorum* of political economy. It remains an insoluble puzzle to most minds, as, although they perceive Mill's reasoning to be irrefutable, they can not get rid of the conviction that it really makes no difference, in the amount of labor that finds employment, whether it is employed directly by themselves or by the funds that they turn over to others.

The proposition is enunciated in the following passage, Book I, chapter v, section 9, of Mill's work:

"We now pass to a fourth fundamental theorem respecting capital, which is, perhaps, oftener overlooked or misconceived than even any of the foregoing. What supports and employs productive labor is the capital expended in setting it to work, and not the demand of purchasers for the produce of the labor when completed. Demand for commodities is not demand for labor. The demand for commodities determines in what particular branch of production the labor and capital shall be employed; it determines the direction of the labor, but not the more or less of the labor itself, or of the maintenance or payment of the labor. These depend on the amount of the capital or other funds directly devoted to the sustenance and remuneration of labor.

"Suppose, for instance, that there is a demand for velvet; a fund ready to be laid out in buying velvet, but no capital to establish the manufacture. It is of no consequence how great the demand may be, unless capital is attracted into the occupation, there will be no velvet made, and consequently none bought; unless, indeed, the desire of the intending purchaser for it is so strong that he employs part of the price he would have paid for it in making advances to work-people, that they may employ themselves in making velvet; that is, unless he converts part of his income into capital, and invest that capital in the manufacture. Let us now reverse the hypothesis, and suppose that there is plenty of capital ready for making velvet, but no demand. Velvet will not be made; but there is no particular preference on the part of capital for making velvet. Manufacturers and their laborers do not produce for the pleasure of their customers, but for the supply of their own wants, and having still the capital and the labor which are the essentials of production, they can either produce something else which is in demand, or, if there be no other demand, they themselves have one, and can produce the things which they want for their own consumption. So that the employment afforded to labor does not depend on the purchasers, but on the capital. I am, of course, not taking into consideration the effects of a sudden change. If the demand ceases unexpectedly after the commodity to supply it is already produced, this introduces a different element into the question; the capital has actually been consumed in producing something which nobody wants or uses, and it has therefore perished, and the employment which it gave to labor is at an end, not because there is no longer a demand, but because there is no longer a capital. This case, therefore, does not test the principle. The proper test is to suppose that the change is gradual and foreseen, and is attended with no waste of capital, the manufacture being discontinued by merely not replacing the machinery as it wears out, and not reinvesting the money as it comes in from the sale of the produce. The capital is thus ready for a new employment, in which it will maintain as much labor as before. The manufacturer and his work-people lose the benefit of the skill and knowledge which they had acquired in the particular business, and which can only be partially of use to them in any other; and that is the amount of loss to the community by the change. But the laborers can still work, and the capital which previously employed them will, either in the same hands or by being lent to others, employ either those laborers or an equivalent number in some other occupation.

"This theorem—that to purchase produce is not to employ labor; that the demand for labor is constituted by the wages which precede the production, and not by the demand which may exist for the commodities resulting from the production—is a proposition which greatly needs all the illustration it can receive. It is, to common apprehension, a paradox; and even among political economists of reputation, I can hardly point to any, except Mr. Ricardo and M. Say, who have kept it constantly and steadily in view. Almost all others occasionally express themselves as if a person who buys commodities, the produce of labor, was an employer of labor, and created a demand for it as really, and in the same sense, as if he bought the labor itself directly by the payment of wages. It is no wonder that political economy advances slowly when such a question as this still remains open at its very threshold. I apprehend that if by demand for labor be meant the demand by which wages are raised, or the number of laborers in employment increased, demand for commodities does not constitute demand for labor. I conceive that a person who buys commodities and consumes them himself does no good to the laboring classes; and that it is only by what he abstains from consuming and expends in direct payments to laborers in exchange for labor, that he benefits the laboring classes or adds anything to the amount of their employment.

"For the better illustration of the principle, let us put the following case: A consumer may expend his income either in buying services or commodities. He may employ part of it in hiring journeymen brick-layers to build a house, or excavators to dig artificial lakes, or laborers to make plantations and lay out pleasure-grounds; or, instead of this, he may expend the same value in buying velvet and laces. The question is, whether the difference between these two modes of expending his income affects the interest of the laboring classes. It is plain that in the first of the two cases he employs laborers who will be out of employment, or, at least, out of that employment in the opposite case. But those from whom I differ say that this is of no consequence, because in buying velvet and lace he equally employs laborers, namely, those who make the velvet and lace. I contend, however, that in this last case he does not employ laborers; but merely decides in what kind of work some other person shall employ them. The consumer does not, with his own funds, pay to the weavers and lace-makers their day's wages. He buys the finished commodity, which has been produced by labor and capital, the labor not being paid nor the capital furnished by him, but by the manufacturer. Suppose that he had been in the habit of expending this portion of his income in hiring journeymen brick-layers, who laid out the amount of their wages in food and clothing, which were also produced by labor and capital. He, however, determined to prefer velvet, for which he thus creates an extra demand. This demand can not be satisfied without an extra capital; where, then, is the capital to come from? There is nothing in the consumer's change of purpose which makes the capital of the country greater than it otherwise was. It appears, then, that the increased demand for velvet could not for the present be supplied were it not that the very circumstance which gave rise to it has set at liberty a capital of the exact amount required. The very sum which the consumer now employs in buying velvet, formerly passed into the hands of journeymen brick-layers, who expended it in food and necessaries, which they now either go without, or squeeze by their competition from the shares of other laborers. The labor and capital, therefore, which formerly produced necessaries for the use of these brick-layers are deprived of their market, and must look out for other employment; and they find it in making velvet for the new demand. I do not mean that the very same labor and capital which produced the necessaries turn themselves to producing the velvet; but, in some one or other of a hundred modes, they take the place of that which does. There was capital in existence to do one of two things—to make the velvet, or to produce necessaries for the journeymen brick-layers; but not to do both. It was at the option of the customer which of the two should happen; and if he chooses the velvet, they go without the necessaries.

"For further illustration, let us suppose the same case reversed. The consumer has been accustomed to buy velvet, but resolves to discontinue that expense, and to employ the same annual sum in hiring brick-layers. If the common opinion be correct, this change in the mode of his expenditure gives no additional employment to labor, but only transfers employment from velvet-makers to brick-layers. On closer inspection, however, it will be seen that there is an increase of the total sum applied to the remuneration of labor. The velvet manufacturer, supposing him aware of the diminished demand for his commodity, diminishes the production and sets at liberty a corresponding portion of the capital employed in the manufacture. This capital, thus withdrawn from the maintenance of velvet-makers, is not the same fund with that which the customer employs in maintaining brick-layers; it is a second fund. There are, therefore, two funds to be employed in the maintenance and remuneration of labor, where before there was only one. There is not a transfer of employment from velvet-makers to brick-layers; there is a new employment created for brick-layers, and a transfer of employment from velvet-makers to some other laborers, most probably those who produce the food and other things which the brick-layers consume.

"In answer to this it is said that the money laid out in buying velvet is not capital, it replaces capital; that, though it does not create a new demand for labor, it is the necessary means of enabling the existing demands to be kept up. The funds (it may be said) of the manufacturer, while locked up in velvet, can not be directly applied to the maintenance of labor; they do not begin to constitute a demand for labor until the velvet is sold, and the capital which made it replaced from the outlay of the purchaser; and thus, it may be said, the velvet-maker and the velvet-buyer have not two capitals, but only one capital between them, which by the act of purchase the buyer transfers to the manufacturer; and if, instead of buying velvet, he buys labor, he simply transfers this capital elsewhere, extinguishing as much demand for labor in one quarter as he creates in another.

"The premises of this argument are not denied. To set free a capital which would otherwise be locked up in a form useless for the support of labor is, no doubt, the same thing to the interests of laborers as the creation of a new capital. It is perfectly true that if I expend £1,000 in buying velvet, I enable the manufacturer to employ £1,000 in the maintenance of labor, which could not have been so employed while the velvet remained unsold; and if it would have remained unsold for ever unless I bought it, then by changing my purpose and hiring brick-layers instead, I undoubtedly create no new demand for labor, for while I employ £1,000 in hiring labor on the one hand, I annihilate for ever £1,000 of the velvet-maker's capital on the other. But this is confounding the effects arising from the mere suddenness of a change with the effects of the change itself. If, when the buyer ceased to purchase, the capital employed in making velvet for his use necessarily perished, then his expending the same amount in hiring brick-layers would be no creation, but merely a transfer of employment. The increased employment which I contend is given to labor, would not be given unless the capital of the velvet-maker could be liberated, and would not be given until it was liberated. But every one knows that the capital invested in an employment can be withdrawn from it, if sufficient time be allowed. If the velvet-maker had previous notice, by not receiving the usual order, he will have produced £1,000 less velvet, and an equivalent portion of his capital will have been already set free. If he had no previous notice, and the article consequently remains on his hands, the increase of his stock will induce him next year to suspend or diminish his production until the surplus is carried off. When this process is complete, the manufacturer will find himself as rich as before, with undiminished power of employing labor in general, though a portion of his capital will now be employed in maintaining some other kind of it. Until this adjustment has taken place, the demand for labor will be merely changed, not increased; but, as soon as it has taken place, the demand for labor is increased. Where there was formerly only capital employed in maintaining weavers to make £1,000 worth of velvet, there is now that same capital employed in making something else, and £1,000 distributed among brick-layers besides. There are now two capitals employed in remunerating two sets of laborers, while before one of those capitals, that of the customer, only served as a wheel in the machinery by which the other capital, that of the manufacturer, carried on its employment of labor from year to year.

"The proposition for which I am contending is in reality equivalent to the following, which to some minds will appear a truism, though to others it is a paradox: that a person does good to laborers, not by what he consumes on himself, but solely by what he does not so consume. If, instead of laying out £100 in wine or silk, I expend it in wages, the demand for commodities is precisely equal in both cases; in the one it is the demand for £100 worth of wine or silk; in the other, for the same value of bread, beer, laborers' clothing, fuel, and indulgences: but the laborers of the community have in the latter case the value of £100 more of the produce of the community distributed among them. I have consumed that much less, and made over my consuming power to them. If it were not so, my having consumed less would not leave more to be consumed by others, which is a manifest contradiction. When less is not produced, what one person forbears to consume is necessarily added to the share of those to whom he transfers his power of purchase. In the case supposed I do not necessarily consume less ultimately, since the laborers whom I pay may build a house for me, or make something else for my future consumption. But I have at all events postponed my consumption, and have turned over part of my share of the present produce of the community to the laborers. If after an interval I am indemnified, it is not from existing produce, but from a subsequent addition made to it. I have therefore left more of the existing produce to be consumed by others; and have put into the possession of laborers the power to consume it."

That the demand for commodities is not a demand for labor as here enunciated assumes that productive consumption can take the place of unproductive indefinitely, while the truth is, it can only do so for a limited period, and must be followed by a comparative increase of unproductive, equal or greater in amount, usually the latter. Let us vary Mill's illustration by supposing the demand of the individual possessing £1,000 to be for a house to live in, and that he will decide to buy a house, or build for himself, according as either action will most benefit the laboring classes. If he decides to buy, his demand in principle is the same as if he expended the one thousand pounds for velvet. If he decides to build, he undoubtedly gives additional employment to labor at the time. But if the society in which he lives is increasing in capital faster than in population, or will do so at some future time, sooner or later, somewhere in the land, a house will not be built which would have been built if he had not anticipated such action. If, at the time he builds, houses are already in excess, the house that he would have bought if he had not built will remain unoccupied, or will serve by lowering rentals as a discouragement to others building, and he will only have anticipated the demand for labor by a very short interval. If there happens to be a scarcity of houses, his building one lessens that scarcity and will prevent others supplying it by just one house. He has then only anticipated the demand for labor, but by a somewhat less interval than when houses are plenty. He can not at all increase the wages-fund, taking one year with another, by his decision between buying and building. He can, however, benefit the situation of the laboring class by equalizing in some slight degree the demand for labor, which he could effect by building in depressed and by buying in prosperous times. The contrary, however, is the usual course of those desiring houses, as they are prone to buy in depressed and build in prosperous times, because they find an individual profit in so doing.

The proposition that the demand for commodities is not a demand for labor has therefore little or no significance, but is merely a verbal distinction, utterly unworthy of the prominence it has attained, and has no bearing in any way or shape on the arguments here advanced, except as such arguments afford the solution of the puzzle. If, however, instead of a house or any other article of prolonged consumption possessed of exchangeable value, the owner of the one thousand pounds employs labor to produce objects of no utility—as, for instance, if he employed them in removing and then bringing back a pile of bricks —he would benefit the laboring class at his own expense. His expenditure would be purely of the nature of a gift to his employés; likewise, if he employs labor in personal services the utility of which perishes in the doing, he certainly adds to the wages-fund. But even then he makes no permanent addition to it, nor does he when his expenditure is of the nature of a gift, even when the funds he expends come from dead stock, or from active stock the product of which was destined by him to serve as capital. If he restricts his own unproductive consumption to obtain, in lieu of it, personal service, he disturbs the normal ratio between capital and population; as the amount of capital remains the same, while the number of laborers seeking employment is less by the number of them employed by him. This results in a rise of proportional wages and fall of profits, which leads to a decline of productive consumption until the ratio is adjusted, and there is for a time less employment for laborers than if he had expended the one thousand pounds unproductively. If his demand for services is permanent, population remaining the same, there is a permanent decline in the normal amount of capital, and the nation is permanently poorer in accumulated wealth than it would have been if his expenditure had been for unproductive consumption of material things. This permanent loss will be to the detriment, not of the rate but of the gross amount of profits, and the wages-fund will be as large as, but no larger than, before.

If the one thousand pounds be taken from capital or from funds which would have been added to capital, our supposed employer of labor in services would lessen equally the amount of capital and the number of productive laborers, except to the degree in which he disturbed the normal ratio of fixed to circulating capital; i. e., labor employed in personal services requiring no fixed capital to speak of, the same amount of capital would employ more labor than before, which would entail some slight decline in profits, and the employment of labor. As before, the community at large will be able to retain somewhat less of capitalized wealth, while the wages-fund will be unaffected.

Every diversion of labor from productive to unproductive employment necessarily decreases the number of laborers productively engaged and *the amount of capital that can be utilized—and can not, as Mill practically claims, at all increase the total number or remuneration of laborers employed productively and unproductively.*

If Mill is right in claiming that the demand for commodities is not a demand for labor, it would follow that the greater the demand for services the better the condition of the laborer should be. During feudal times this demand was very much greater than it has ever since been, but the rates of both proportional and real wages were then normally lower than at present, and no one will claim that a return to feudal customs would now be of any benefit to laborers, nor that it would not certainly lead to an enormous decrease in capitalized wealth, and the annual product of material things. The appeal to facts, therefore, is decidedly against Mill's ingenious theory.

The world can elect what proportion of its labor shall be utilized productively, and what in services, but it can not increase the amount of services and enjoy the same amount of material products as before; and this, when analyzed, is what the proposition, that the demand for commodities is not a demand for labor, really asserts.

Certain economists propose to include services under the term "wealth." To this misuse of language I can not agree; not that I deny that services possess exchangeable value, but because the distinction between material and immaterial things is too radical. The latter can neither be accumulated nor distributed, and the discovery of the laws governing the accumulation and distribution of material wealth is the chief object of the science. As we have seen, services, although not themselves material things, nevertheless affect the production and accumulation of material things, and possess as well both value and utility. They come certainly under the cognizance of the science, but as causes, not effects. They themselves stand in but little need of explanation, but aid in explaining what does.

CHAPTER III.

THE TENDENCY OF CAPITAL TO OUTSTRIP POPULATION.

I HAVE now reached the more agreeable task of showing that my views of the nature and limits of capital differ from those of Mill and Ricardo mainly in the manner of statement, and are not essentially diverse. I do, indeed, object most strenuously to the way in which they present the subject; as I hold that it prevents in great part the practical application of economic ideas, and leads these great thinkers, as we shall see later on, to several erroneous theoretical conclusions. I may be pardoned if I quote somewhat more extensively than the argument strictly calls for, on account of my personal anxiety to be considered rather as supplementing than as supplanting their contributions to the science.

To commence, then, with Mill, I will first quote from Book I, chapter xi, section 3:

"When a country has carried production as far as in the existing state of knowledge it can be carried, with an amount of return corresponding to the average strength of the effective desire of accumulation in that country, it has reached what is called the stationary state—the state in which no further addition will be made to capital unless there takes place either some improvement in the arts of production, or an increase in the strength of the desire to accumulate. In the stationary state, though capital does not on the whole increase, some persons grow richer and others poorer. Those whose degree of providence is below the usual standard, become impoverished, their capital perishes, and makes room for the savings of those whose effective desire of accumulation exceeds the average. These become the natural purchasers of the land, manufactories, and other instruments of production owned by their less provident countrymen."

Also from Book IV, chapter iv, section 5:

"I now say that the mere continuance of the present annual increase of capital, if no circumstance occurred to counteract its effect, would suffice in a small number of years to reduce the rate of net profit to one per cent.

"To fulfill the conditions of the hypothesis, we must suppose an entire cessation of the exportation of capital for foreign investment. No more capital sent abroad for railways or loans; no more emigrants taking capital with them to the colonies, or to other countries; no fresh advances made, or credits given, by bankers or merchants to their foreign correspondents. We must also assume that there are no fresh loans for unproductive expenditure by the government, or on mortgage, or otherwise; and none of the waste of capital which now takes place by the failure of undertakings, which people are tempted to engage in by the hope of a better income than can be obtained in safe paths at the present habitually low rate of profit. We must suppose the entire savings of the community to be annually invested in really productive employment within the country itself; and no new channels opened by industrial inventions, or by a more extensive substitution of the best-known processes for inferior ones.

"Few persons would hesitate to say that there would be great difficulty in finding remunerative employment every year for so much new capital, and most would conclude that there would be what used to be termed a general glut; that commodities would be produced, and remain unsold, or be sold only at a loss. But the full examination which we have already given to this question has shown that this is not the mode in which the inconvenience would be experienced. The difficulty would not consist in any want of market. If the new capital were duly shared with many varieties of employment, it would raise up a demand for its own produce, and there would be no cause why any part of that produce should remain longer on hand than formerly. What would really be, not merely difficult, but impossible, would be to employ this capital without submitting to a rapid deduction of the rate of profit.

"As capital increased, population either would also increase, or it would not. If it did not, wages would rise, and a greater capital would be distributed in wages among the same number of laborers. There being no more labor than before, and no improvements to render the labor more efficient, there would not be any increase of the produce; and as the capital, however largely increased, would only obtain the same gross return, the whole savings of each year would be exactly so much subtracted from the profits of the next and of every following year. It is hardly necessary to say that in some circumstances profits would very soon fall to the point at which further increase of capital would cease. *An augmentation of capital, much more rapid than that of population, must soon reach its extreme limit*, unless accompanied by increased efficiency of labor (through inventions and discoveries, or improved mental and physical education), or unless some of the idle people, or of the unproductive laborers, became productive."

And, again, from Book I, chapter xiii, section 1:

"But there are other countries, and England is at the head of them, in which neither the spirit of industry nor the effective desire of accumulation need any encouragement; where the people will toil hard for a small remuneration, and save much for a small profit; where, though the general thriftiness of the laboring class is much below what is desirable, *the spirit of accumulation in the more prosperous part of the community requires abatement rather than increase.* In these countries there would never be any deficiency of capital, if its increase were never checked or brought to a stand by too great a diminution of its returns."

And from Book IV, chapter v, section 1:

"It must always have been seen, more or less distinctly, by political economists, that the increase of wealth is not boundless; that at the end of what they term the progressive state lies the stationary state; that all progress in wealth is but a postponement of this, and that each step in advance is an approach to it. *We have now been led to recognize that this ultimate goal is at all times near enough to be fully in view;* that we are always on the verge of it, and that, if we have not reached it long ago, it is because the goal itself flies before us. The richest and most prosperous countries would very soon attain the stationary state, if no further improvements were made in the productive arts, and if there were a suspension of the overflow of capital from those countries into the uncultivated or ill-cultivated regions of the earth."

And from Book V, chapter iv, section 4:

"In England the great emigration of capital, and the almost periodical occurrence of commercial crises through the speculations occasioned by the habitually low rate of profit, are indications that profit has attained the practical though not the ultimate minimum, and that all the savings which take place (beyond what improvements, tending to the cheapening of necessaries, make room for) are either sent abroad for investment or periodically swept away."

To this I must object that no destruction of capital or wealth in any form occurs during a panic. The excess of capital is not "*swept away*" in any sense of the term. It is not even devoted to unproductive consumption, as that itself in such times is lessened. The readjustment comes, and can only come, from a decrease in productive consumption, greater than the accompanying decrease in unproductive. If unproductive consumption did not decrease, the proper ratio of capital to population would be obtained much sooner than it now is, viz., when production had been decreased to an amount exactly equal to the previous over-accumulation; and the only loss that society would suffer would be what it would have lost if the superabundant capital had been destroyed by fire, or in any manner consumed without affording any enjoyment or satisfaction. But the curtailment of unproductive consumption adds to this loss one of many times its extent, viz., the loss for ever of all those enjoyments which individuals have foregone by lessening their unproductive consumption, in their endeavor to retain their own capital unimpaired; or rather the loss of the production which would have satisfied such unproductive consumption. There is here a case where individual are opposed to social interests. By retrenching expenditure the individual adds to, or at least retains more of, his capital; but he does it at the expense of the capital of his fellow-citizens. The capital that the community can permanently employ, including his own, is actually lessened by his accretions when the general capital has increased more rapidly than population.

Again, in Book I, chapter v, section 7:

"This perpetual consumption and reproduction of capital affords the explanation of what has so often excited wonder, the great rapidity with which countries recover from a state of devastation; the disappearance, in a short time, of all traces of the mischiefs done by earthquakes, floods, hurricanes, and the ravages of war. An enemy lays waste a country by fire and sword, and destroys or carries away nearly all the movable wealth existing in it; all the inhabitants are ruined, and yet, in a few years after, everything is much as it was before. This *vis medicatrix naturæ* has been a subject of sterile astonishment, or has been cited to exemplify the wonderful strength of the principle of saving, which can repair such enormous losses in so brief an interval. There is nothing at all wonderful in the matter. What the enemy have destroyed, would have been destroyed in a little time by the inhabitants themselves; the wealth which they so rapidly reproduce, would have needed to be reproduced and would have been reproduced in any case, and probably in as short a time. Nothing is changed, except that during the reproduction they have not now the advantage of consuming what had been produced previously. *The possibility of a rapid repair of their disasters mainly depends on whether the country has been depopulated. If its effective population have not been extirpated at the time, and are not starved afterward*, then, with the same skill and knowledge which they had before, with their land

and its permanent improvements undestroyed, and the more durable buildings probably unimpaired, or only partially injured, they have nearly all the requisites for their former amount of production. If there is as much of food left to them, or of valuables to buy food, as enables them by any amount of privation to remain alive and in working condition, they will in a short time have raised as great a produce, and acquired collectively as great wealth and as great a capital, as before, by the mere continuance of that ordinary amount of exertion which they are accustomed to employ in their occupations. Nor does this evince any strength in the principle of saving, in the popular sense of the term, since what takes place is not intentional abstinence, but involuntary privation."

And, finally, Book IV, chapter iv, section 4:

"We now arrive at the fundamental proposition which this chapter is intended to inculcate. When a country has long possessed a large production, and a large net income to make savings from, and when, therefore, the means have long existed of making a great annual addition to capital (the country not having, like America, a large reserve of fertile land still unused), it is one of the chief characteristics of such a country, that the rate of profit is habitually within, as it were, a hand's breadth of the minimum, and the country, therefore, on the very verge of the stationary state. By this I do not mean that this state is likely, in any of the great countries of Europe, to be soon actually reached, or that capital does not still yield a profit considerably greater than what is barely sufficient to induce the people of those countries to save and accumulate."

I will also quote Ricardo in this connection, calling attention to the fact that he here uses capital in Mill's sense, and can not mean by it the wages-fund—although most of his assertions are only true of the wages-fund—as no increase of that beyond the increase of population is conceivable.

Ricardo's works, chapter xxi, page 174:

"No accumulation of capital will permanently lower profits, unless there be some permanent cause for the rise in wages. If the funds for the maintenance of labor were doubled, tripled, or quadrupled, there would not long be any difficulty in procuring the necessary number of hands to be employed by those funds, but, owing to the increasing difficulty of making constant additions to the food of the country, funds of the same value would probably not maintain the same quantity of labor. If the necessaries of the workmen could be constantly increased with the same facility, there could be no permanent alteration in the rate of profit or wages, to whatever amount capital might be accumulated. Adam Smith, however, uniformly ascribes the fall of profits to the accumulation of capital, to the competition which will result from it, without ever adverting to the increasing difficulty of providing food for the additional number of laborers which the additional capital will employ. 'The increase of stock,' he says, 'which raises wages tends to lower profits.' Adam Smith speaks here of a rise of wages, but it is a temporary rise proceeding from increased funds before the population is increased, and he does not appear to see that, at the same time that the capital is increased, the work to be effected by capital is increased in the same proportion. M. Say has, however, most satisfactorily shown that there is no amount of capital which may not be employed in a country, because demand is only limited by production. No man produces but with a view to consume or sell, and he never sells but with an intention to purchase some other commodity, which may be immediately useful to him or which may contribute to future production. By producing, then, he necessarily becomes either the consumer of his own goods, or the purchaser and consumer of the goods of some other person.

"There can not then be accumulated in a country any amount of capital which can not be employed productively until wages rise so high in consequence of the rise of necessaries, and so little consequently remains for the profits of stock, that the motive for accumulation ceases.

"Whether these increased productions, and the consequent demand which they occasion, shall or shall not lower profits, depends solely on the rise of wages; and the rise of wages, excepting for a limited period, on the facility of producing the food and necessaries of the laborer; I say for a limited period, because no point is better established than that the supply of laborers will always ultimately be in proportion to the means of supporting them.

"There is only one case, and that will be temporary, in which the accumulation of capital, with a low price of food, may be attended with a fall of profits, and that is, *when the funds for the maintenance of labor increase much more rapidly than population; wages will then be high, and profits low. If every man were to forego the use of luxuries and be intent only on accumulation, a quantity of necessaries might be produced for which there could not be any immediate consumption. Of commodities so limited in number there might undoubtedly be a universal glut*, and consequently there might neither be demand for an additional quantity of such commodities nor profits on the employment of more capital. If men ceased to consume they would cease to produce—this admission does not impugn the general principle."

Without any separate criticism of these quotations, I am justified in asserting that, with much from which I dissent, they contain or imply every one of my premises and deductions, except that of the influence of increase of capital upon population. That the conclusions of Ricardo and Mill differ from mine, is owing solely to their ambiguous use of the term "capital." Every one of the principles I have advocated, with the above exception, they enunciate distinctly, except that they usually, but not always, assume that capital, in Mill's sense, and the wages-fund, i. e., capital, in Ricardo's sense, vary together; whereas I hold that they vary inversely, other things, of course, remaining the same. In this assertion there can be no doubt that I am right and they wrong; and it is readily seen that they fell into their error from not fully perceiving all the implications of their own definitions of capital, and through taking it for granted that what was true of it in one tense was true of it in all, and from the misleading supposition that a low rate of profit was a stimulus to population.

But I differ from them in a matter I have not yet

touched upon, except by implication, viz., in my views as to what constitutes the progressive, stationary, and retrogressive states of society; and the difference is important, as the soundness of my position here will affect the truth of deductions to be made later on, the practical application of which will profoundly influence the economic policy which nations should adopt to secure for themselves the greatest possible share of the world's products, and to increase to the highest point their own productive efficiency.

The circumstance that seems to me important is the determination of the question whether the net produce of a nation bears an increasing, a decreasing, or a steady ratio to its population. If the income *per capita* of its people is growing larger, I should say it was enjoying an economic progress; if smaller, that it was going backward, irrespective of whether such advance or retrogression was accompanied by a growth or decline of the total wealth and population.* It is, indeed, true that any increase in net income *per capita* is usually accompanied by an increase in the aggregate of accumulation and of population; but the latter must be distinguished from the former as being its effect and counteractant. It is its effect, because any increase in net income is an additional stimulus to population; and its counteractant, because every increase of numbers lowers the margin of cultivation, and because every increase of capital beyond that of population decreases the capacity of the nation to produce by lessening the number of laborers employed: but there is no necessary connection between increase of net income

* In net income I would include the income of immediate satisfactions and enjoyments derived from commodities reserved for prolonged unproductive consumption, as well as of those derived from services.

and population, or between a large annual production and accumulation. When people understand and fully appreciate the working of economic laws, they will endeavor to dissociate them, and there is no reason why they should be unsuccessful in such efforts. When this is effected, advantages gained in productive efficiency will not be wasted in a mere increase of numbers, or be frittered away and made barren of enjoyment by the attempt to possess more capitalized wealth than economic law allows.

Strictly speaking, there is no stationary state of society at all. The perpetual flux and reflux of human events prevent such a state from being more than momentary, a mere turning-point between the progressive and the retrogressive, or *vice versa*. When the growth in net incomes, in which I consider the progressive state to consist, is counteracted by the growth of aggregate capital and population, which Mill seems to consider as constituting it, society pauses stationary for a moment, and then enters the retrogressive state, in which its annual produce and net income decline, and this proceeds until the consequent decrease of capital and population checks society in its downward course, and it again momentarily pauses, in a second and lower stationary state, from which an advance is once more effected. If, on the whole, a nation progresses in wealth, population, and the average income of its inhabitants (without this last ingredient, I refuse to accept it as progress at all), it is not, as Mill seems to suppose, because it has never entered the stationary or retrogressive states, but because its passage through the progressive state has been longer, and has more influenced its economic condition, than its passage through the others. The progress of society is due, not to ground never being lost, but to the fact that, while much is repeatedly lost, more has been gained: like the incoming tide, each wave has reached a higher level than its predecessor.

Mill, and Ricardo with him, seems to have considered the stationary state of society as never practically reached, and to have thought it somewhat problematical that it ever would be. They would both freely admit the conclusions I have drawn, as well as those to be hereafter deduced, as applicable to such a social condition, and, when induced to admit that all civilized nations complete the round of the three states in constantly recurring periods of about ten years, they could not but regard the validity of my conclusions as established. The possibility of capital pressing upon population is clearly recognized by them. If they had recognized that this pressure is not only an abstract possibility, but an actually existent economic fact, and that the pressure of capital upon population is as constant and steady as that of population upon the food-supply, they could not have failed to draw as important conclusions from the principle they neglected, as being merely theoretical, as they did draw from the theory of Malthus.

That the tendency of capital to increase faster than population is steady and constant, whenever and wherever men in their economic actions are undisturbed by abnormal events, is the central thought of this treatise, and is the contribution I bring to the science of political economy.

I do not mean by this that capital constantly increases more rapidly than population, any more than Malthus meant that population always increased faster than its food-supply. The increase of capital and of population both have their checks, which operate in very similar manner.

Profits are the means of support to capital, as truly and very much in the same sense as food is the means of support to population. The checks upon both capital and population operate in the same manner, and not only often forbid further increase, but sometimes demand an actual decrease. It is not the increase of either population or capital that is constant, but the *tendency* to such increase *beyond their economic limits*.

I must not be understood as asserting that all human societies show this tendency in a periodical increase of capital beyond the needs of population. Whenever and wherever capital is physically insufficient to furnish the amount of wages-fund that can be profitably employed, the limitations to capital are removed as long as such condition lasts. In one sense all barbarous, semi-civilized, and despotic countries, where there is but scanty security for life and property, can be said to be in this condition, and the checks to accumulation in them are moral and social, and not economic. What I mean is, that in the absence of war, famine, and bad government, capital will constantly tend to outstrip population, will periodically succeed in so doing, and will be in excess, to the detriment of production for a greater or less portion of the time. The analogy between the pressure it exerts and that exerted by population on the margin of cultivation is as perfect as it is the nature of any analogy to be. Even taking Mill's definition of what constitutes the stationary state, viz., the decline of the rate of profit to the minimum and the cessation of accumulation, what is more evident than that such decline is the most important occurrence in every period of industrial stagnation, and that not only in such times is the stationary state as defined by him reached, but that the rate of profit then declines below the minimum and carries the community for a time into the retrogressive state in which a decrease of production takes place? That the state of civilized communities is still on the average progressive, is certainly no proof that the other states are not occasionally reached. A permanent stationary or retrogressive state can not occur until all the fertile land of the globe is reclaimed, and then only in the absence of further improvements and inventions, and of a decrease of population, except, indeed, population increases as fast as, or faster than, the reclamation of fertile land. The condition of mankind in the stationary and retrogressive states, instead, however, of being a curious problem, the solution of which has a practical interest for future generations alone, is a topic of pressing importance.

CHAPTER IV.

FIXED CAPITAL.

"There is a great difference between the effects of circulating and those of fixed capital, on the amount of the gross produce of the country. Circulating capital being destroyed as such, or at any rate finally lost to the owner, by a single use, and the product resulting from that one use being the only source from which the owner can replace the capital, or obtain any remuneration for its productive employment, the product must of course be sufficient for those purposes; or, in other words, the result of a single use must be a reproduction equal to the whole amount of the circulating capital used, and a profit besides. This, however, is by no means necessary in the case of fixed capital. Since machinery, for example, is not wholly consumed by one use, it is not necessary that it should be wholly replaced from the product of that use. The machine answers the purpose of its owner, if it brings in, during each interval of time, enough to cover the expense of repairs, and the deterioration in value which the machine has sustained during the same time, with a surplus sufficient to yield the ordinary profit on the entire value of the machine.

"*From this it follows that all increase of fixed capital, when taking place at the expense of circulating, must be at least temporarily prejudicial to the interests of the laborers.* This is true, not of machinery alone, but of all improvements by which capital is sunk; that is, rendered permanently incapable of being applied to the maintenance and remuneration of labor. Suppose that a person farms his own land, with a capital of two thousand quarters of corn, employed in maintaining laborers during one year (for simplicity we omit the consideration of seed and tools), whose labor produces him annually two thousand four hundred quarters, being a profit of twenty per cent. This profit we shall suppose that he annually consumes, carrying on his operations from year to year on the original capital of two thousand quarters. Let us now suppose that, by the expenditure of half his capital, he effects a permanent improvement of his land, which is executed by half his laborers, and occupies them for a year, after which he will only require, for the effectual cultivation of his land, half as many laborers as before. The remainder of his capital he employs as usual. In the first year there is no difference in the condition of the laborers, except that part of them have received the same pay for an operation on the land which they previously obtained for plowing, sowing, and reaping. At the end of the year, however, the improver has not, as before, a capital of two thousand quarters of corn. Only one thousand quarters of his capital have been reproduced in the usual way: he has now only those thousand quarters and his improvements. He will employ, in the next and in each following year, only half the number of laborers, and will divide among them only half the former quantity of subsistence. The loss will soon be made up to them if the improved land, with the diminished quantity of labor, produces two thousand four hundred quarters as before, because so enormous an accession of gain will probably induce the improver to save a part, add it to his capital, and become a larger employer of labor. But it is conceivable that this may not be the case; for (supposing, as we may do, that the improvement will last indefinitely, without any outlay worth mentioning to keep it up) the improver will have gained largely by his improvement if the land now yields, not two thousand four hundred, but one thousand five hundred quarters; since this will replace the one thousand quarters forming his present circulating capital, with a profit of twenty-five per cent (instead of twenty as before) on the whole capital, fixed and circulating together. The improvement, therefore, may be a very profitable one to him, and yet very injurious to the laborers.

"The supposition, in the terms in which it has been stated, is purely ideal; or at most applicable only to such a case as that of the conversion of arable land into pasture, which, though formerly a frequent practice, is regarded by modern agriculturists as the reverse of an improvement. The clearing away of the small farmers in the north of Scotland, within the present century, was, however, a case of it; and Ireland, since the potato famine and the repeal of the corn-laws, is another. The remarkable decrease which has lately attracted notice in the gross produce of Irish agriculture is, to all appearance, partly attributable to the diversion of land from maintaining human laborers to feeding cattle; and it could not have taken place without the removal of a large part of the Irish population by emigration or death. We have thus two recent instances in which what was regarded as an agricultural improvement has diminished the power of the country to support its population. The effect, however, of all the improvements due to modern science is to increase, or, at all events, not to diminish, the gross produce. But this does not affect the substance of the argument. Suppose that the improvement does not operate in the manner supposed—does not enable a part of the labor previously employed on the land to be dispensed with—but only enables the same labor to raise a greater produce. Suppose, too, that the greater produce, which by means of the improvement can be raised from the soil with the same labor, is all wanted, and will find purchasers. The improver will in that case require the same number of laborers as before, at the same wages. But where will he find the means of paying them? He has no longer his original capital of two thousand quarters disposable for the purpose. One thousand of them are lost and gone—consumed in making the improvement. If he is to employ as many laborers as before, and pay them as highly, he must borrow, or obtain from some other source, a thousand quarters to supply the deficit. But these thousand quarters already maintained, or were destined to maintain, an equivalent quantity of labor. They are not a fresh creation; their destination is only changed from one productive employment to another; and, though the agriculturist has made up the deficiency in his own circulating capital, the breach in the circulating capital of the community remains unrepaired."—(Mill, Book I, chapter vi, section 2.)

The necessity which the English school of economists labor under, of making it appear that industrial inactivity is due to the scarcity of material wealth, or rather of circulating capital, has led them to assert that the increase of fixed capital often causes the decrease of the wages-fund. They generally express themselves somewhat differently, and substitute the words "circulating capital" for wages-fund; as, in the above passage, Mill says: "From this it follows that all increase of fixed capital, when taking place at the expense of circulating, must be, at least temporarily, prejudicial to the interests of the laborers." The passage is not true, unless circulating capital is understood as the wages-fund alone. It sometimes happens that the increase of fixed capital is at the expense of the wages-fund, and Mill gives two instances where this has occurred; but it is evident that such depletion of the wages-fund can not occur until the other part of circulating capital—dead stock—is first converted into fixed capital. But Mill evidently intends to convey the idea that all increase of fixed, at the expense of circulating capital (as defined by himself), is prejudicial to the laborers. On the contrary, it is evident that any depletion of dead stock by its conversion into fixed capital raises the rate of profit on active circulating stock, and leads to a further depletion of dead stock by the conversion of more of it into the wages-fund than would otherwise go there. The demand for labor resulting from the conversion of dead stock into fixed capital can not raise real, though it may money, wages, because while it is taking place the decrease of dead stock will cause the things in which wages are really paid to rise in money-value more than money-wages can by any possibility advance. What finally causes a rise in wages and a decline in the money-value of dead stock is, the demand for labor caused by the attempt to utilize such fixed capital; and such rise of wages and fall in the value, as compared with wages, of dead stock, can only occur when the labor at first applied to the creation of fixed capital is employed in utilizing it in production, and *has caused an increase of dead stock to such degree as to more than make up its depletion by fixed capital.*

Over-investment, even when it is so great as to use up all the dead and part of the active stock besides, puts off the time when labor can not be profitably employed. Its action is that of an anticipated demand for labor, and its evil effects are not felt until the period of recuperation; then the demand that has been anticipated can not be exerted. The idle factories and workshops stand ready to be utilized the moment there is a profit in using them; and no more will be erected until their number becomes insufficient for the demands of industry. If, in times of stagnation, all superfluous fixed capital and dead stock were incontinently destroyed, it would lead to an almost immediate resumption of industrial activity. If this were habitually done, it would be greatly to the advantage of the laborers, as it would result in a permanent increase of the average amount of the wages-fund. Nor would it be at all to the disadvantage of capitalists as a class; on the contrary, they would gain by it, though not to the extent of the laborers. The real destruction of such property occurs when funds that should have gone to unproductive consumption were diverted to fixed capital, or retained as dead stock. Once suffered, the loss is irreparable; but a further loss is entailed to both labor and capital by the continuance in existence of such property, prohibiting future production often to many times its own amount. I am not advocating any destruction of unprofitable stock; that would certainly be impracticable without entailing great injustice to individuals; but I am pleading against its creation. Such arbitrary destruction of superabundant capital does sometimes occur in the natural course of human events, and is always followed by a season of great industrial activity. This explains the rapid recovary of nations from the effects of the most devastating wars, and their prosperity during their continuance, although the destruction of human life and the drain of laborers to the army largely counteract the effects of the depletion of capital. Witness the wonderful recovery of France from the terrible losses and enormous indemnity imposed upon her by Germany. Germany brought home with her milliards her own industrial ruin, and has undergone a loss in productive power many times greater than the sum she filched from her neighbor, while France is wealthier to-day than before the enormous tribute was exacted.

It is incorrect, therefore, to attribute the origin of our depressions to over-investment. What that really effects is, to defer their occurrence, and to prolong them when finally they do occur.

That Mill's views really coincide with mine, as expressed in this chapter, I also claim, and submit the following extracts to prove the assertion, and shall leave them without further comment than the intelligent reader can supply for himself from what has been said, and will only ask that Mill's ambiguous use of the term "capital" shall be constantly borne in mind:

"The theory of the effect of accumulation on profits laid down in the preceding chapter, materially alters many of the practical conclusions which might otherwise be supposed to follow from the general principles of political economy, and which were, indeed, long admitted as true by the highest authorities on the subject.

"It must greatly abate, or rather, altogether destroy, in countries where profits are low, the immense importance which used to be attached by political economists to the effects which an event or a measure of government might have in adding to, or subtracting from, the capital of the country. We have now seen that the lowness of profits is a proof that the spirit of accumulation is so active, and that the increase of capital has proceeded at so rapid a rate, as to outstrip the two counter-agencies, improvements in production, and increased supply of cheap necessaries from abroad: and that unless a considerable portion of the annual increase of capital were either periodically destroyed, or exported for foreign investment, the country would speedily attain the point at which further accumulation would cease; or, at least, spontaneously slacken so as no longer to overpass the march of invention in the arts which produce the necessaries of life. In such a state of things as this, a sudden addition to the capital of the country, unaccompanied by any increase of productive power, would be but of transitory duration; since by depressing profits and interest, it would either diminish by a corresponding amount the savings which would be made from income in the year or two following, or it would cause an equivalent amount to be sent abroad, or to be wasted in rash speculations. Neither, on the other hand, would a sudden abstraction of capital, unless of inordinate amount, have any real effect in impoverishing the country. After a few months or years, there would exist in the country just as much capital as if none had been taken away. The abstraction, by raising profits and interest, would give a fresh stimulus to the accumulative principle, which would speedily fill up the vacuum. Probably, indeed, the only effect that would ensue, would be that for some time afterward less capital would be exported, and less thrown away in hazardous speculation.

"In the first place, then, this view of things greatly weakens, in a wealthy and industrious country, the force of the economical argument against the expenditure of public money for really valuable, even though industriously unproductive, purposes. If for any great object of justice or philanthropic policy, such as the industrial regeneration of Ireland, or a comprehensive measure of colonization or of public education, it were proposed to raise a large sum by way of loan, politicians need not demur to the abstraction of so much capital as tending to dry up the permanent sources of the country's wealth, and diminish the fund which supplies the subsistence of the laboring population. The utmost expense which could be requisite for any of these purposes would not, in all probability, deprive one laborer of employment, or diminish the next year's production by one ell of cloth or one bushel of grain. In poor countries, the capital of the country requires the legislator's sedulous care; he is bound to be most cautious of encroaching upon it, and should favor to the utmost its accumulation at home, and its introduction from abroad. But in rich, populous, and highly cultivated countries, it is not capital which is the deficient element, but fertile land; and what the legislator should desire and promote, is not a greater aggregate saving, but a greater return to savings, either by improved cultivation, or by access to the produce of more fertile lands in other parts of the globe. In such countries, the government may take any moderate portion of the capital of the country and expend it as revenue, without affecting the national weath, the whole being either drawn from that portion of the annual savings which would otherwise be sent abroad, or being subtracted from the unproductive expenditure of individuals for the next year or two, since every million spent makes room for another million to be saved before reaching the overflowing point. When the object in view is worth the sacrifice of such an amount of the expenditure that furnishes the daily enjoyments of the people, the only well-grounded economical objection against taking the necessary funds directly from capital, consists of the inconveniences attending the process of raising a revenue by taxation, to pay the interest of a debt.

"The same considerations enable us to throw aside as unworthy of regard one of the common arguments against emigration as a means of relief for the laboring class. Emigration, it is said, can do no good to the laborers, if, in order to defray the cost, as much must be taken away from the capital of the country as from its population. That anything like this proportion could require to be abstracted from capital for the purpose even of the most extensive colonization, few, I should think, would now assert; but, even on that untenable supposition, it is an error to suppose that no benefit would be conferred on the laboring class. If one tenth of the laboring people of England were transferred to the colonies, and along with them one tenth of the circulating capital of the country, either wages or profits, or both, would be greatly benefited, by the diminished pressure of capital and population upon the fertility of the land. There would be a reduced demand for food; the inferior arable lands would be thrown out of cultivation, and would become pasture; the superior would be cultivated less highly, but with a greater proportional return; food would be lowered in price, and, though money-wages would not rise, every laborer would be considerably improved in circumstances—an improvement which, if no increased stimulus to population and fall of wages ensued, would be permanent; while, if there did, profits would rise, and accumulation start forward so as to repair the loss of capital. The landlords alone would sustain some loss of income; and even they, only if colonization went to the length of actually diminishing capital and population, but not if it merely carried off the annual increase.

"From the same principles we are now able to arrive at a final conclusion respecting the effects which machinery, and generally the sinking of capital for a productive purpose, produce upon the immediate and ultimate interests of the laboring class. The characteristic property of this class of industrial improvements is the conversion of circulating capital into fixed; and it was shown, in the first book, that, in a country where capital accumulates slowly, the introduction of machinery, permanent improvements of land, and the like, might be, for the time, extremely injurious; since the capital so employed might be directly taken from the wages-fund, the subsistence of the people and the employment for labor curtailed, and the gross annual produce of the country actually diminished. But, in a country of great annual savings and low profits, no such effects need be apprehended. Since even the emigration of capital, or its unproductive expenditure, or its absolute waste, do not in such a country, if confined within any moderate bounds, at all diminish the aggregate amount of the wages-fund, still less can the mere conversion of a like sum into fixed capital, which continues to be productive, have that effect. It merely draws off at one orifice what was already flowing out at another; or, if not, the greater vacant space left in the reservoir does but cause a greater quantity to flow in. Accordingly, in spite of the mischievous derangements of the money-market which have been occasioned by the sinking of great sums in railways, I was never able to agree with those who apprehended mischief from this source to the productive resources of the country. Not on the absurd ground (which to any one acquainted with the elements of the subject needs no confutation) that railway expenditure is a mere transfer of capital from hand to hand, by which nothing is lost or destroyed. This is true of what is spent in the purchase of the land; a portion, too, of what is paid to parliamentary agents, counsel, engineers, and surveyors, is saved by those who receive it, and becomes capital again; but what is laid out in the *bona fide* construction of the railway itself is lost and gone; when once expended, it is incapable of ever being paid in wages or applied to the maintenance of laborers again; as a matter of account, the result is that so much food and clothing and tools have been consumed, and the country has got a railway instead. But what I would urge is, that sums so applied are mostly a mere appropriation of the annual overflowing which would otherwise have gone abroad, or been thrown away unprofitably, leaving neither a railway nor any other tangible result. The railway gambling of 1844 and 1845 probably saved the country from a depression of profits and interest, and a rise of all public and private securities, which would have engendered still wilder speculations, and, when the effects came afterward to be complicated by the scarcity of food, would have ended in a still more formidable crisis than was experienced in the years immediately following. In the poorer countries of Europe, the rage for railway construction might have had worse consequences than in England, were it not that in those countries such enterprises are in a great measure carried on by foreign capital. The railway operations of the various nations of the world may be looked upon as a sort of competition for the overflowing capital of the countries where profit is low and capital abundant, as England and Holland. The English railway speculations are a struggle to keep our annual increase of capital at home; those of foreign countries are an effort to obtain it.*

"It already appears from these considerations that the conversion of circulating capital into fixed, whether by railways, or manufactories, or ships, or machinery, or canals, or mines, or works of drainage and irrigation, is not likely, in any rich country, to diminish the gross produce or the amount of employment for labor. How much, then, is the case strengthened, when we consider that these transformations of capital are of the nature of improvements in production, which, instead of ultimately diminishing circulating

* It is hardly needful to point out how fully the remarks in the text have been verified by subsequent facts. The capital of the country, far from having been in any degree impaired by the large amount sunk in railway construction, was soon again overflowing.

capital, are the necessary conditions of its increase; since they alone enable a country to possess a constantly augmenting capital, without reducing profits to the rate which would cause accumulation to stop! There is barely any increase of fixed capital which does not enable the country to contain eventually a larger circulating capital than it otherwise could possess and employ within its own limits; for there is hardly any creation of fixed capital which, when it proves successful, does not cheapen the articles on which wages are habitually expended.

"Nevertheless, I do not believe that, as things are actually transacted, improvements in production are often, if ever, injurious, even temporarily, to the laboring classes in the aggregate. They would be so if they took place suddenly to a great amount, because much of the capital sunk must necessarily in that case be provided from funds already employed as circulating capital. But improvements are always introduced very gradually, and are seldom or never made by withdrawing circulating capital from actual production, but are made by the employment of the annual increase. *There are few, if any, examples of a great increase of fixed capital, at a time and place where circulating capital was not rapidly increasing likewise.* It is not in poor or backward countries that great and costly improvements in production are made. To sink capital in land for a permanent return, to introduce expensive machinery, are acts involving immediate sacrifice for distant objects, and indicate, in the first place, tolerably complete security of property; in the second, considerable activity of industrial enterprise; and, in the third, a high standard of what has been called the 'effective desire of accumulation'—which three things are the elements of a society rapidly progressive in its amount of capital. Although, therefore, the laboring classes must suffer, not only if the increase of fixed capital takes place at the expense of circulating, but even if it is so large and rapid as to retard that ordinary increase to which the growth of population has habitually adapted itself; yet, in point of fact, this is very unlikely to happen, since there is probably no country whose fixed capital increases in a ratio more than proportional to its circulating. If the whole of the railways which, during the speculative madness of 1845, obtained the sanction of Parliament, had been constructed in the times fixed for the completion of each, this improbable contingency would, most likely, have been realized;

but this very case has afforded a striking example of the difficulties which oppose the diversion into new channels of any considerable portion of the capital that supplies the old; difficulties generally much more than sufficient to prevent enterprises that involve the sinking of capital from extending themselves with such rapidity as to impair the sources of the existing employment for labor.

"To these considerations must be added that, even if improvements did for a time decrease the aggregate produce and the circulating capital of the community, they would not the less tend, in the long run, to augment both. They increase the return to capital; and of this increase the benefit must necessarily accrue either to the capitalist in greater profits, or to the customer in diminished prices; affording in either case an augmented fund from which accumulation may be made, while enlarged profits also hold out an increased inducement to accumulation."—(Mill, Book IV, chapter v, sections 1 and 3.)

One criticism is perhaps advisable on the last quotation. Mill says, "There are few, if any, examples of a great increase of fixed capital at a time and place where circulating capital was not rapidly increasing likewise." As he defines capital, this is hardly true: using the word according to Ricardo, it is true, because, as I have shown, the transfer of dead circulating capital to the fixed form is the cause of an additional amount of dead circulating capital being also transferred to the fund of active circulating capital, and that it is true in this sense is an important verification of the principles here advanced.

The immediate effect of the creation of fixed capital in sustaining profits by its depletion of dead stock might seem to be partially counteracted by its withdrawing laborers from the production of circulating stock. The greater competition for labor resulting, undoubtedly tends to raise proportional wages, and would do so were it not that the demand for productive and unproductive consumption remaining the same while the supply of commodities to be consumed being, by the supposition, decreased, the relative value of labor is lowered as compared with other commodities, fixed capital excepted.

The case is the same when previously unemployed labor is used in the creation of fixed capital; this necessitates an increase in the demand for productive and unproductive consumption together, while there is no increase in the supply of commodities to be consumed. This can only result in a fall in proportional wages and increase of the rate of profit. This is what always occurs during the periods when fixed capital is being created, as, even when it diverts labor from other production, other production utilizes the unemployed labor of the community. As the process, however, causes a constant decline in the relative value of fixed capital, such periods of inflated prosperity and activity are soon brought to an end by the creation of fixed property ceasing to be profitable.

CHAPTER V.

PANICS.

That the current explanations of panics are not very satisfactory, will be conceded by most students of our science. We have seen already that a conclusive test exists, and can be applied, to disprove the most common and popular one advanced, viz., that they are due to the depletion of capital resulting from the waste and extravagance of the prosperous times that precede them. The popular apprehension of the subject is that they are mainly due to this cause, and the mass of their readers peruse with approval the diatribes of our newspaper economists, denouncing expenditure both public and private. Such readers are very sure that, individually, they increase their incomes through saving, and lessen them through spending; and it is naturally hard for them to understand why the same is not true of themselves collectively.

Economists, however, being somewhat more given to verifying theory by fact, have, to a very considerable extent, recognized that the seasons of "waste and extravagance," being also those of great productive efficiency, are, despite the large expenditure, the seasons in which alone the community saves and adds to its wealth. Accepting the authority of Mill and Ricardo, that increase of wealth must lead to an increase of the wages-fund and of production, they recognize the discrepancy of theory and fact, and attempt to account for it mainly by an endeavor to explain away the fact. They say that it is not wealth, but only a part of wealth, that employs labor, and that the decrease of employment is due to the depletion of such part (circulating capital) by a diversion of the funds, that should have flowed into it, to permanent investment (fixed capital). But we have already seen that this explanation is the reverse of true, as not the whole of circulating capital, but only a part of it, employs labor, and that such part is not only relatively but absolutely the smaller, population remaining the same, when circulating capital in gross is the greatest; and we have also seen that the creation of fixed capital, by decreasing dead stock, always tends to a corresponding increase of the active stock of circulating capital, or of the wages-fund. It must, therefore, be acknowledged that, on the occurrence of a crisis, the funds *physically available* for the employment of labor, and the material wealth of the community in every form, are greater than at other times.

Mill himself is wiser than his followers. Confused though he was by his ambiguous use of the term "capital," he nevertheless perceived that accumulations were greatest just before a crisis, but, deceived by his erroneous use of the term "market," he was unwilling to acknowledge, in apparent contradiction to Say, that accumulation tended to prevent exchanges; and he attempts to explain crises as referable solely to the action of the credit system. In Book III, chapter xiv, section 4, he says:

"But it is a great error to suppose, with Sismondi, that a commercial crisis is the effect of a general excess of production." (It is excess of accumulation, not of production, contended against in this treatise, and practically contended for by Mill.) "It is simply the consequence of an excess of speculative purchases. It is not a gradual advent of low prices, but a sudden recoil from prices extravagantly high. Its immediate cause is a contraction of credit, and the remedy is not a *diminution of supply*, but the restoration of confidence."

Nothing could be more unequivocal than this, and nothing could be more in contradiction to it than the following passage in Book IV, chapter iv, sections 5 and 6:

"What, then, are these counteracting circumstances, which, in the existing state of things, maintain a tolerably equal struggle against the downward tendency of profits, and prevent the great annual savings which take place in this country from depressing the rate of profit much nearer to that lowest point to which it is always tending, and which, left to itself, it would so promptly attain? The resisting agencies are of several kinds.

"First among them we may notice one which is so simple and so conspicuous that some political economists, especially M. de Sismondi and Dr. Chalmers, have attended to it almost to the exclusion of all others. This is, the waste of capital in periods of overtrading and rash speculation, and in the commercial revulsions by which such times are always followed. It is true that a great part of what is lost at such periods is not destroyed, but merely transferred, like a gambler's losses, to more successful speculators. But even of these mere transfers a large portion is always to foreigners, by the hasty purchase of unusual quantities of foreign goods at advanced prices. And much also is absolutely wasted. Mines are opened, railways or bridges made, and many other works of uncertain profit commenced, and in these enterprises much capital is sunk which yields either no return, or none adequate to the outlay. Factories are built and machinery erected beyond what the market requires, or can keep in employment. Even if they are kept in employment, the capital is no less sunk; it has been converted from circulating into fixed capital, and has ceased to have any influence on wages or profits." (We have seen that Mill is mistaken in assuming that the amount of fixed capital has no influence on wages.) "*Besides this, there is a great unproductive consumption of capital, during the stagnation which follows a period of general overtrading. Establishments are shut up, or kept working without any profit, hands are discharged, and numbers of persons in all ranks, being deprived of their income, and thrown for support on their savings, find themselves, after the crisis has passed away, in a condition of more or less impoverishment. Such are the effects of a commercial revulsion: and that such revulsions are almost periodical is a consequence of the very tendency of profits which we are considering. By the time a few years have passed over without a crisis, so much additional capital has been accumulated that it is no longer possible to invest it at the accustomed profit:* all public securities rise to a high price, the rate of interest on the best mercantile security falls very low, and the complaint is general among persons in business that no money is to be made. Does not this demonstrate how speedily profit would be at the minimum, and the stationary condition of capital would be attained, if these accumulations went on without any counteracting principle? But the diminished scale of all safe gains inclines persons to give a ready ear to any projects which hold out, though at the risk of loss, the hope of a higher rate of profit; and speculations ensue, which, with the subsequent revulsions, destroy or transfer to foreigners a considerable amount of capital, produce a temporary rise of interest and profit, make room for fresh accumulations, and the same round is recommenced.

"This, doubtless, is one considerable cause which arrests profits in their descent to the minimum, by sweeping away, from time to time, a part of the accumulated mass by which they are forced down. But this is not, as might be inferred from the language of some writers, the principal cause. If it were, the capital of the country would not increase; but in England it does increase greatly and rapidly. This is shown by the increasing productiveness of almost all taxes, by the continual growth of all the signs of national wealth, and by the rapid increase of population, while the condition of the laborers is certainly not declining, but, on the whole, improving. These things prove that each commercial revulsion, however disastrous, is very far from destroying all the capital which has been added to the accumulations of the country since the last revulsion preceding it, and that invariably room is either found or made for the profitable employment of a perpetually increasing capital, consistently with not forcing down profits to a lower rate.

"This brings us to the second of the counter-agencies, namely, improvements in production. These evidently have the effect of extending what Mr. Wakefield terms the field of employment, that is, they enable a greater amount of capital to be accumulated and employed without depressing the rate of profit—provided always that they do not raise to a proportional extent the habits and requirements of the laborer.

"If the laboring class gain the full advantage of the increased cheapness—in other words, if money-wages do not fall—profits are not raised, nor their fall retarded. But if the laborers people up to the improvement of their condition, and so relapse to their previous state, profits will rise. All inventions which cheapen any of the things consumed by the laborers, unless their requirements are raised in an equivalent degree, in time lower money-wages; and, by doing so, enable a greater capital to be accumulated and employed before profits fall back to what they were previously."

When Mill says that "the remedy is not a diminution of supply," he is right, if by remedy he means prevention. The evil has not been caused by any excess of production, but by the non-utilization, in either productive or unproductive consumption, of too great a portion of what has been produced. If he means that it is not the proper remedy after the crisis has occurred, he is right only if he means to advocate, which he is far from doing, the absolute destruction or unproductive consumption of excessive dead stock. But, as this will seldom take place naturally, the diminution of supply, undesirable as it is, is the only remedy the undisturbed action of economic law supplies, and the sole means by which the readjustment of capital to population is in practice effected. There is too self-evident an appeal to facts for this to be denied, nor does Mill deny it, contradictory as it is to his assertion, but explicitly asserts it in the passage which I have italicized in the last quotation.

But I further assert that credit is never a cause of crises at all, but only an accelerating influence, by which I mean that, as prices would then be stationary or nearly so, a crisis could never occur from any extension of credit not accompanied by over-accumulation; while the latter would periodically produce seasons of industrial inactivity, even if business were conducted on a strictly cash basis. In saying this, I, of course, do not mean to assert that credit is without influence. Its influence is undeniably great, and the larger part of the losses society sustains through its enforced periods of industrial inactivity must be attributed to it. All that I contend for is, that it must be considered only as intensifying effects due to over-accumulation, and that would not occur at all without over-accumulation.

Gold and silver, leaving out of view their use as commodities, subserve a double purpose. They act as the standard of value, and as the medium of exchange. If they had never been supplemented by credit, their value would be many times greater than it now is.

"Having now formed a general idea of the modes in which credit is made available as a substitute for money, we have to consider in what manner the use of these substitutes affects the value of money, or, what is equivalent, the prices of commodities. It is hardly necessary to say that the permanent value of money—the natural and average prices of commodities—are not in question here. These are determined by the cost of producing or of obtaining the precious metals. An ounce of gold or silver will, in the long run, exchange for as much of every other commodity as can be produced or imported at the same cost with itself; and an order or note of hand, or bill payable at sight, for an ounce of gold, while the credit of the giver is unimpaired, is worth neither more nor less than the gold itself."—(Mill, Book III, chapter xii, section 1.)

Nevertheless, credit does permanently affect the value of gold, because it affects the amount needed. Every time (other things remaining the same) credit supplies the function of gold in exchange, it depresses its value. If the value sinks below the cost of production, the value of gold is not thereby eventually raised, but the cost of production is itself lowered by the abandonment of some of the poorer mines. If credit did not exist, we should have more gold and silver, and they would be of greater value. While their production would have been greatly stimulated, and while we would possess several times the amount we do now, the money prices of other articles would be but a small fraction of what they are now. The introduction of credit has rendered unnecessary a great amount of labor that would otherwise have been expended in their production, and has saved a very considerable loss that would have occurred through their greater destruction by accident and wear. It has also yielded a further gain in the convenience, or lessened labor, by means of which exchanges are effected.

What concerns us more nearly, however, is the effect of credit upon prices, and through them upon production, consumption, and accumulation. Credit, no matter what its form, does not increase capital, but it does increase the availability or effectiveness of capital. It facilitates exchange, stimulates production, and places the existent capital in the hands of those most disposed to make investments—thus leading to a more rapid accumulation. But, in the end, supposing the same state of civilization to be reached without it as with it, it decreases the possible accumulation of capital, both because of the smaller amounts of the precious metals that the community will accumulate, and because a smaller amount of more available capital will suffice for the needs of production—that is, under the credit system—as capital will be more active, a smaller amount will be needed; and the normal ratio of capital to population will be lessened. Besides the economies already noticed, the credit system confers a benefit upon society in that it lessens the relative amount of savings and investments that the growing needs of society demand.

If gold and silver were our only mediums of exchange, the fluctuations in prices, that depend upon their relative amount, would be greater than they now are. Any increased demand upon them as mediums of exchange may now be partly met by an extension of credit, or an improvement in its methods which may carry the community over the period of their relative scarcity without much depressing prices. The production of the precious metals is very variable in amount, but the effect of their greater or less production upon prices is largely modified by the credit system, because it now performs the greater portion of their functions, and in so doing possesses an elasticity which specie does not, because the latter can only increase in its amount, when the demand for it is great, through importation of the precious metals or by the slow process of greater activity in mining, whereas credit expands of itself with every fresh demand upon it as a medium of exchange, without much affecting prices. The fluctuations in prices, that depend upon the greater or less activity of exchanges, would be much less if we had no system of credit. The demand upon gold and silver, if we depended upon them alone, resulting from any increase of prices or unusual activity of exchanges would be immediately felt, and the value of the precious metals relative to other commodities increased, which is to say that the prices of other commodities would soon fall, and the activity of exchanges be checked; whereas under the credit system the increase of credit that always accompanies an increase in the activity of exchanges helps to sustain prices. As the fluctuations that depend upon the activity of exchanges are vastly more numerous than those depending upon the abundance or scarcity of the precious metals, it is evident that fluctuations are very much more frequent, sudden, and greater in amount, under the credit system.

While it allows greater latitude for fluctuation in prices, any extension of credit, no matter what its form—whether it be an increase of currency, an extension of bank credits, or the greater facility with which time-purchases are made—raises the prices of all commodities, not only by the creation of a greater demand, but by its disturbance of the ratio of the amount of the commodities to the amount of their medium of exchange. That is to say, the increase of credit tends to raise prices by depreciating the value of the medium through which commodities are exchanged, and also to raise them through the stimulation of demand that results from the additional facility it gives to exchange and production.

Any rise in prices is primarily and mainly a benefit to the capitalist, who possesses the commodity enhanced in value. It is a profit to him additional to the legitimate return for the use of capital he was before receiving for producing or transferring that commodity. Such profit represents no gain of any kind to the community, but only a transfer from the pocket of the consumer to the pocket of the capitalist exactly equal to the increase in the price of the commodity. A general rise in prices simply means that capital receives a larger, and labor a smaller, proportion of the total production, than they were receiving before it took place. As such rise always stimulates production, the amount to be divided is greater, and the absolute share of the laborers may be, and usually is, larger than before; but their relative share is less. Capital receives the larger share of the benefit of the increased activity.

We see, therefore, that the effect of the credit system, when it commences to act upon a normal ratio of capital to population, is to stimulate prices and increase profits, and to hasten the over-accumulations that are inevitably made from excessive profits, and which necessitate a following period of inactivity and decline.

But it has a further effect. Not only does the credit system shorten the rhythm of activity and idleness, but it renders the fluctuations more variable in their effect upon individuals. If every article were paid for by its purchaser at the moment of purchase, the benefits of a general rise in prices would be distributed among all the holders of property, each of whom would gain a slight increase of wealth; but, when the articles enhanced in value have certain fixed claims against them, the proportional benefit to their possessors is thereby increased. A rise in price of ten per cent gives an extra profit of ten per cent on articles fully paid for; but if half the purchase-money is yet due, the profit is twenty per cent on the possessor's real interest in them. When credits are very much extended, a rise in prices, instead of making small additions to many incomes, makes larger additions to fewer incomes. The larger sudden additions to incomes are, the larger will be the proportion of them that will be invested, and the smaller will be the increase of expenditure. Thus, again, we find that credit hastens over-accumulation.

Having now reached the top of the wave, we will follow it over the crest to its decline. Higher prices can only be maintained when they are the result of permanent causes, and such causes must not only be permanent but world-wide. There are such causes, and they can all be resolved into the permanent increase of the proportion which the medium of exchange, whether gold or credit, bears to the amount of commodities seeking exchange. The world has experienced such an increase for several centuries and still continues to experience it. It has been, and is, both a cause and result of advancing civilization. But any permanent advance in prices must not only proceed from permanent causes, but from causes that equally affect those portions of the civilized world that exchange any considerable proportion of their production with others. When any single nation, by increasing its medium of exchange, or from any other cause, raises the money prices of its commodities more than its neighbors, it immediately places itself at a disadvantage as compared with them; and they are enabled to undersell it in both its own and foreign markets. The productions of a nation so situated must accumulate within its own borders. It will also accumulate foreign productions, which will commence to occupy its home market. Such a nation is finally forced to reduce its production. Until it does so its imports will exceed its exports; or, in other words, it will borrow of other nations, and must pay a portion of its income to them as interest. If it does not pay the balance due, in gold and silver, and its creditors do not choose to make a permanent investment of their advances, the rate of exchange, or the equation of international demand, will be against it, which again places it at a commercial disadvantage. If they do permanently invest such advances, foreign capital is brought into competition with home capital at the very time that excessive profits and investments have made capital superabundant. The only escape from the inevitable result of this state of things is the general reduction of prices. The higher and more rapid their rise has been, the lower and more sudden their fall must be.

But this fall is no more a loss to the community than their rise was a gain. The property of the community is exactly what it was when every one was apparently wealthy. Like the rise, the decline is a mere transfer of values; but now it is the consumer who gains, and the capitalist who loses. The only loss to the nation is on the relatively small portion of the production it exports, as its gain in the rise was also on its exports. This loss is trivial, and is balanced by a previous fictitious gain. The real injury to the community is the very serious loss of its labor, forced to be idle during the period of depression.

The effect of credit on this transfer of value is to distribute the loss in a manner very different from its natural proportions. If there were no indebtedness, the losses consequent upon the fall in prices would be distributed *pro rata* among all the possessors of commodities. But if, as before supposed, these possessors were indebted for half the purchase value of their goods, the loss to them is doubled, while the lenders lose nothing unless the decline is so great as to invalidate their security.

If this loss were distributed as evenly as it would be if the credit system did not exist, it would cause little suffering and no alarm, because no one could become insolvent. The worst that any would suffer, would be a slight reduction of capital and income, to which they could readily adjust their affairs. But the loss being concentrated upon a few, who are indebted in certain fixed sums, it renders so many of them insolvent, that lenders, becoming alarmed for the adequacy of their security, contract credits as much and as suddenly as they possibly can. Now, this process not only forces a further decline in prices, by stopping all the demand that proceeds from investment, but also by forcing holders of property to sell at any price, in order to obtain means for the repayment of indebtedness for which they can no longer obtain credit. It also forces prices down, by lessening the proportion of the medium of exchange to the amount of commodities seeking exchange. The fearful disturbance of the social organism that the severity of this process causes has been too vividly experienced by us all to need further elucidation. We have merely to remark that the effect of the credit system is to depress prices in a time of depression more than they otherwise would be, as well as to raise them in times of prosperity higher than they would otherwise go. Neither their rise nor fall is a gain or a loss to the community; but the widening of the fluctuations is an evil, in that it increases the idleness, or loss of labor, which is the real and only injury that panics cause.

But prices in any nation can no more be kept permanently below prices in other nations than they can be kept above them; nor can they long be kept at a point that forbids profit. The loss being merely a transfer from the property to the consuming classes, the consuming power of the latter, though absolutely less, is, relatively to production, greater than before. Over-accumulations cease—profits being too small to allow them to be made. Exports once more exceed imports; the suffering nation, again able to produce as cheaply as, or cheaper than, its neighbors, repays its foreign indebtedness, and resumes its control of home and foreign markets, and the rate of exchange and the equation of international demand are again in its favor. The nation re-enters upon a period of prosperity and advancing prices, in which it proceeds with accelerating progress, again to suffer from its economic mistake of endeavoring to be richer than economic law allows.

We are now entitled to state that panics are the sudden and violent readjustment from an abnormal to a normal ratio of capital to population. Their cause is solely the disturbance of this ratio. The only effect of the credit system is to accelerate the rhythm and increase the extent of the fluctuations above and below the point at which the ratio harmonizes with the present state of society.

If the large profits resulting from a rise in prices were expended wholly for productive and unproductive consumption, and did not result in any increase of "dead stock" either fixed or circulating, the rise of price would be maintained, for the efficient demand would always equal the supply, however great the latter might be, and production would continue to be as profitable as before. There would be, to be sure, a redistribution of wealth, but, as long as the ratio of capital to population was not really disturbed, further fluctuations in general prices would be only such as would result from false suppositions that the ratio was disturbed. As further investments would not be made, or, if made, would continue to be profitable because their amount would be strictly proportional to the increase of population, a collapse of credit, however extended it might be, could hardly occur, for confidence could not be shaken when it was felt that dead stock was not in excess. Such a balance of population and capital is of course chimerical. It is too ideal a state of society to be hoped for or expected. It is quite within the province of reason, however, to show that some approximation to it is possible, and that its full attainment would free us for ever from commercial crises.

As the result of our investigations, we are also entitled to state that the benefits we derive from the credit system—when the point has been reached in a nation's history at which a tendency to over-accumulation begins to show itself—can all be resolved into the reduction of the proportion which capital normally bears to population; and its evils, into the intensification of the temporary fluctuations it causes in the ratio of capital to population.

The permanent rise in prices which, as before explained, we owe to the credit system, may perhaps be considered as an exception to this remark. Any permanent advance of the point about which prices tend to fluctuate prolongs the period of large profits in which it takes place, without prolonging the following period of reaction. It would seem, therefore, that it must also increase the totality of production, and the augmentation of capital such increase of production demands and justifies. We have seen, however, that this is not an advantage, unless the totality of unproductive consumption is also increased. That it does this is not so clear, but may still, we think, be asserted. Increase of production is always attended by some increase of consumption; but the proportion between the two is much less disturbed by a gradual than by a sudden rise of prices. A sudden increase of income will yield a larger percentage for investment than a gradual one of equal extent. The more gradual it is, the closer will the increased expenditure approximate to the increased income, and, if it be very gradual, may almost or quite equal it. Now, this permanent rise in prices is very gradual, having extended over several centuries, and it has undoubtedly been wholly utilized in unproductive consumption, and not wasted in uncalled-for saving. But, if this explanation is the true one, this benefit which we derive from credit is analogous to the others, in that it results from an increase of unproductive consumption, without any more than a corresponding and fit increase of capital.

Our principle has now afforded us a reasonably full and accurate explanation of the cause and action of panics as affecting individual nations. It might seem, at first sight, that, where all nations advanced with nearly equal rapidity, and at the same time, toward higher prices and more extended credits, the result would be a permanent rise of prices from which no reaction could possibly follow. Steam and electricity are making one commercial community of the nations. Economic relations are now so intimate and so sensitive, that we may hereafter expect that the alternations of activity and stagnation will become more and more uniform, both in extent and time, for all communities. As two vibrating chords, when brought together, tend to vibrate in unison, so the commercial rhythms of separate nations tend to uniformity as distances are annihilated. This uniformity of rhythm, in proportion as it is perfect, removes the restraint upon each other's inflation of credit and prices which has been hitherto exercised. But it never can be perfect, and always will allow some portion of the restraining influence to be exerted. Although it may lengthen the rhythm of activity and idleness, it can never destroy it, but will rather tend to its intensification. We may expect these states, when more universal, to be longer in their continuance and more extreme in their intensity; but they will continue as before in all other respects. Their real, indeed their only, cause is over-accumulation. The only difference is, that the relief from their burden is longer deferred, and more tedious when commenced, where the difficulty of distributing the over-accumulations among foreign nations is enhanced. This can not be done so effectively where all are suffering, in nearly equal degree, from the same cause.

It has hitherto been claimed that a "general glut" was impossible; that the world could not have too much of everything. But facts are stubborn things, and something very like it has come to pass. A general glut is the result, not, as Mill assumes, of over-production, but of over-accumulation; and we have seen, not only that this is possible, but that the tendency of society toward such a state is constant so long as it possesses an undue proportion of the accumulating class. We have also seen that the credit system intensifies the tendency to over-accumulation, both in its beneficial effect of lessening the necessary proportion of capital to population and in its evil tendencies of stimulating the fluctuation of prices, and confining the consequent gains and losses to fewer individuals without lessening their amount. All these causes act over the whole area as certainly and as systematically as over any particular portion. The only difference that their universal rhythm makes to any particular nation is, that it takes away, to the extent in which it occurs, the opportunity of relieving the home markets by exporting the surplus which is depressing them, to other nations that will not or can not take it when they are oppressed in like degree with a superabundance of dead stock. Except as modified by this one circumstance, the readjustment of capital to population proceeds exactly the same when the periods of alternating activity and stagnation coincide as when they are independent. The cause of panic and depression is not in the least altered by the periodical coincidence of industrial activity. Decline in prices and production must follow over-accumulation, and collapse of credit must follow decline in prices, so long as the consequent transfer of property from the capitalist to the consumer is at the expense of a few of the capitalists, instead of being distributed *pro rata* among them.

The loss of confidence which constitutes the essential nature of panic as distinguished from stagnation can only result from the anticipation of a decline in prices. But a decline in prices can only be effected by a decrease in the medium of exchange or an increase in the amount of commodities to be exchanged; the latter cause can only result from over-accumulation, and the former from a destruction or exportation of the precious metals. The fact that in any nation prices are higher than in the rest of the world will lead to such exportation, and also if speculation at any time should raise prices above the level determined by the ratio of commodities to the medium of exchange, so that production was yielding more than its normal rate of profit, an exportation of gold would take place sufficient to soon reduce prices and profits to the normal rate. This fall in prices, when anticipated, would cause, undoubtedly, some loss of confidence, but, if at the time the proportion of capital to population was not too large, the rate of profit could not fall to a point that would materially decrease production.

In an isolated nation which neither imported nor exported gold, general prices would be wholly governed by the increase or decrease of capital as compared with population. Speculation would affect particular not general prices, and that only temporarily. The amount of production, within certain limits never practically reached, would be strictly inverse to the amount of accumulation; and it is hardly conceivable that any disturbance of confidence and credit, not proceeding from an abnormal cause, such as war, could lead to any considerable cessation of industry, as long as capital continued barely sufficient for the needs of population. Nothing that could be dignified with the name of a commercial crisis could occur as long as production was sufficiently profitable. The world as a whole must be considered as an isolated nation, and no disturbance of credit and confidence can therefore be a sufficient cause for a world-wide depression. That cause can only be found in general over-accumulation. When, therefore, I claimed over-accumulation as the sole cause of commercial crises I meant general, not national crises. The latter may be brought about by the exportation of gold, but can never be very severe if the normal ratio of capital to population has not been too much disturbed.

My arguments, if valid, surely supply the only satisfactory explanation of commercial crises ever advanced; and that they do so is certainly an important verification of the deductions made, and entitle them to more consideration than similar ideas have heretofore received. There has been, indeed, much excuse for the neglect and even the contempt with which somewhat similar views have been regarded, as they have heretofore been presented in language, apparently at least, subversive of many of the best-established results of the science. I have labored, I hope not without success, to show that they are really in accord with the ideas and results of the best thinkers, and that these themselves, as well as their less able opponents, are not free from confusion in their use of terms, and that, when inaccuracies of statement and definition are removed, the views of those on both sides of the dispute are seen to coincide with results, as we shall see later on, in the practical application of the science, as well as in its theories, contemplated by neither.

CHAPTER VI.

CREDIT.

Although not so strictly in the line of our argument, some criticisms upon Mill's view of credit will be advisable, as his accuracy of statement and clearness of perception on the subject have been somewhat impaired by his ambiguous conception of what constitutes the loanable fund.

In Book II, chapter xv, section 4, he says:

"There is scarcely any dealer or producer on a considerable scale, who confines his business to what can be carried on by his own funds. When trade is good, he not only uses to the utmost his own capital, but employs in addition much of the credit which that capital obtains for him. When, either from over-supply or from some slackening in the demand for his commodity, he finds that it sells more slowly or obtains a lower price, he contracts his operations, and does not apply to bankers or other money-dealers for a renewal of their advances to the same extent as before. A business which is increasing holds out, on the contrary, a prospect of profitable employment for a larger amount of this floating capital than previously, and those engaged in it become applicants to the money-dealers for larger advances, which, from their improving circumstances, they have no difficulty in obtaining. A different distribution of floating capital between two employments has as much effect in restoring their profits to an equilibrium as if the owners of an equal amount of capital were to abandon the one trade and carry their capital into the other. This easy, and as it were spontaneous, method of accommodating production to demand is quite sufficient to correct any inequalities arising from the fluctuations of trade, or other causes of ordinary occurrence."

If Mill had been a merchant, he could hardly have failed to see that the process he here explains is not what really occurs.

When goods accumulate, and trade becomes poor, the demand for loans increases, they being evidently needed by the producer to enable him "to carry" his goods; or, if he has parted with them to a speculator or jobber, they will need loans to the same extent, except as they employ their own capital for the purpose; but this is equivalent to the other, as thereby the same amount of funds is removed from the loan market. The number of discounts in such times will be less, because that depends largely upon the activity of exchange, which is then much reduced; but the amount on loan, or withdrawn from the loan market to carry unsalable goods, will be larger than ever, and will be greater in those trades in which the greatest accumulations have taken place and which are consequently the dullest. When, on the contrary, any particular trade is brisk, the amount that will be loaned to it, for the purpose of carrying its dead stock, will be small. When, however, the profits of any trade are so large as to lead to new investments of fixed capital in it, its demand for loans will increase, both because to some extent such investments will be made from borrowed funds, and because, when made by those belonging to the owners, they remove an equivalent amount of funds from the loan market. An active trade demands more active stock but less dead stock than a depressed one, and usually, indeed, we may say always, depends less for its circulating capital upon the loan market. In active times, the decrease in the demand for loans to carry dead stock is greater than the increase of loans to be employed productively, and any increase in the amount on loan must be attributed to the demand for purposes of fixed investment; except, indeed, shortly before a crisis occurs, when, the amount of dead stock having greatly increased and nearly reached its limit, large loans will also be needed to carry it. In active times, therefore, a great increase of the amount on loan is a sign that accumulation is rapidly approaching its limit, and that a reaction may soon be expected.

In Book III, chapter xxiii, section 3, Mill says:

"I have, thus far, considered loans, and the rate of interest, as a matter which concerns capital in general, in direct opposition to the popular notion, according to which it only concerns money. In loans, as in all other money transactions, I have regarded the money which passes, only as the medium, and commodities as the thing really transferred—the real subject of the transaction. And this is, in the main, correct; because the purpose for which, in the ordinary course of affairs, money is borrowed, is to acquire a purchasing power over commodities. In an industrious and commercial country, the ulterior intention commonly is, to employ the commodities as capital; but even in the case of loans for unproductive consumption, as those of spendthrifts, or of the government, the amount borrowed is taken from a previous accumulation, which would otherwise have been lent to carry on productive industry; it is, therefore, so much subtracted from what may correctly be called the amount of loanable capital.

"There is, however, a not unfrequent case, in which the purpose of the borrower is different from what I have here supposed. He may borrow money, neither to employ it as capital nor to spend it unproductively, but to pay a previous debt. In this case, what he wants is not purchasing power, but legal tender, or something which a creditor will accept as equivalent to it. His need is specifically for money, not for commodities or capital. It is the demand arising from this cause which produces almost all the great and sudden variations of the rate of interest. Such a demand forms one of the earliest features of a commercial crisis. At such a period, many persons in business, who have contracted engagements, have been prevented by a change of circumstances from obtaining in time the means on which they calculated for fulfilling them. These means they must obtain at any sacrifice, or submit to bankruptcy; and what they must have is money. Other capital, however much of it they may possess, can not answer the purpose unless money can first be obtained for it; while, on the contrary, without any increase of the capital of the country, a mere increase of circulating instruments of credit (be they of as little worth for any other purpose as the box of one-pound notes discovered in the vaults of the Bank of England during the panic of 1825) will effectually serve their turn, if only they are allowed to make use of it. An increased issue of notes, in the form of loans, is all that is required to satisfy the demand, and put an end to the accompanying panic. But, although in this case it is not capital or purchasing power that the borrower needs, but money as money, it is not only money that is transferred to him. The money carries its purchasing power with it wherever it goes; and money thrown into the loan market really does, through its purchasing power, turn over an increased portion of the capital of the country into the direction of loans. Though money alone was wanted, capital passes; and it may still be said with truth that it is by an addition to loanable capital that the rise of the rate of interest is met and corrected.

"Independently of this, however, there is a real relation, which it is indispensable to recognize, between loans and money. Loanable capital is all of it in the form of money. Capital destined directly for production exists in many forms; but capital must always be such as to adjust these two amounts to one another.* But while

* I do not include in the general loan-fund of the country the capitals, large as they sometimes are, which are habitually employed in speculatively buying and selling the public funds and other securities. It is true that all who buy securities add, for the time, to the general amount of money on loan, and lower, to that extent, the rate of interest. But as the persons I speak of buy only to sell again at a higher price, they are alternately in the position of lenders and borrowers: their operations raise the rate of interest at one time, exactly as much as they lower it at another. Like all persons who buy and sell on speculation, their function is to equalize, not to

the whole of this mass of lent capital takes effect upon the permanent rate of interest, the fluctuations depend almost entirely upon the portion which is in the hands of bankers; for it is that portion almost exclusively which, being lent for short times only, is continually in the market seeking an investment. The capital of those who live on the interest of their own fortunes has generally sought and found some fixed investment, such as the public funds, mortgages, or the bonds of public companies, which investment, except under peculiar temptations or necessities, is not changed.

"Fluctuations in the rate of interest arise from variations either in demand for loans or in the supply. The supply is liable to variation, though less so than the demand. The willingness to lend is greater than usual at the commencement of a period of speculation, and much less than usual during the revulsion which follows. In speculative times money-lenders, as well as other people, are inclined to extend their business by stretching their credit; they lend more than usual (just as other classes of dealers and producers employ more than usual) of capital which does not belong to them. Accordingly, these are the times when the rate of interest is low; though for this, too (as we shall hereafter see), there are other causes. During the revulsion, on the contrary, interest always rises inordinately, because, while there is a most pressing need on the part of many persons to borrow, there is a general disinclination to lend. This disinclination, when at its extreme point, is called a panic. It occurs when a succession of unexpected failures has created, in the mercantile, and sometimes also in the non-mercantile, public, a general distrust in each other's solvency; disposing every one not only to refuse fresh credit, except on very onerous terms, but to call in, if possible, all credit which he has already given. Deposits are withdrawn from banks; notes are returned on the issuers in exchange for specie; bankers raise their rate of discount, and withhold their customary advances; merchants refuse to renew mercantile bills. At such times the most calamitous consequences were formerly experienced, from the attempt of the law to prevent more than a certain limited rate of interest from being given or

raise or lower the value of the commodity. When they speculate prudently, they temper the fluctuations of price; when imprudently, they often aggravate them.

taken. Persons who could not borrow at five per cent had to pay, not six or seven, but ten or fifteen per cent, to compensate the lender for risking the penalties of the law; or had to sell securities or goods for ready money at a still greater sacrifice.

"In the intervals between commercial crises there is usually a tendency in the rate of interest to a progressive decline, from the gradual process of accumulation; which process, in the great commercial countries, is sufficiently rapid to account for the almost periodical recurrence of these fits of speculation; since, when a few years have elapsed without a crisis, and no new and tempting channel for investment has been opened in the mean time, there is always found to have occurred in those few years so large an increase of capital seeking investment as to have lowered considerably the rate of interest, whether indicated by the prices of securities or by the rate of discount on bills; and this diminution of interest tempts the possessor to incur hazards in hopes of a more considerable return."

Mill has, apparently, nowhere attempted to ascertain what portion of the general fund constitutes the loanable fund, but seems to suppose that it is composed of a part only of the general fund. It is evident that the loanable fund is not composed of money, as its sum is many times too large, though Mill seems to imply it by the assertion that it is always in the form of money; as far, indeed, as money is concerned, the loanable fund of a community is only temporarily diminished by a loan being effected. Such loan is very soon deposited by the borrower, and there is as much *money* to lend as before. The amount the community carry in their pockets and the amount in transit may, indeed, vary somewhat, but such variance is trivial in amount, though not in its effects. What, then, constitutes the loanable fund? It is evidently the disposable goods, the capital stock of the community; but what constitutes the demand for loans? It is as evidently the same capital stock that can be given as security. Not that all goods form a part of the demand and of the supply of loanable funds, but, when goods form no part of the one fund, neither do they of the other. When the owner of any commodities is able to carry them without borrowing, they form neither a part of such demand nor supply; it is only when he effects their exchange, or, what is equivalent to exchange, raises a loan upon them as security, that the loan market is affected, and such transaction affects the supply and demand equally. The loan market, then, is as purely a case of reciprocal demand as the general market for commodities, in which, as Say has shown, demand can never exceed supply, or supply demand.

By demand for loans I, of course, mean an efficient demand. The mere desire to borrow is much greater than the desire to lend without adequate security. From personal motives money is sometimes so lent, but, when it is, the desire of the borrower by that very circumstance has become an efficient demand. What is really transferred by a loan is not money, but the use of capital—or, rather, the use of material wealth in the broadest sense of the term, as the lender may, or may not, intend to employ such wealth productively. Now, it is evident that all the wealth of the community can be loaned if its owners are willing to loan it, and others are willing to borrow it of them; but when this was effected there would be no decrease of loanable funds, for the original borrowers could loan it all over again to others, if so disposed.

If by loanable is meant, not, able to be loaned, but, what will be loaned, that amount, of course, will be governed by the inducements held out by borrowers. What those inducements must be will depend mainly upon the exchangeable value of the use of capital, i. e., upon the rate of profit, in operations similarly situated as to difficulty and risk. But such inducement, to be an effectual one, will not have to be at all enhanced on account of any increase in the amount of loans made, except as such increase enhances the risk of lending. The amount of commodities that can be lent is exactly the same, after they are loaned, as before. We are justified in considering the loan of money as a purchase, and its repayment as a repurchase, of the commodities which form the security, and interest as the profit that accrues on the transaction, and, if it is less or more than other profits, it will only be because it entails less or more of risk, trouble, and skill. Independent of these, interest will follow the same law as profits, because it really is a profit.

But there is one radical distinction between profits and interest. Profits rise when prices rise or when money-wages fall, and fall when prices fall and money-wages rise. But a fall in prices is the same as a rise in the value of money. The profit of owning or lending money, therefore, the rate of interest remaining constant, rises when prices are declining, and falls when prices rise. Interest may be very low and the gross profit of owning obligations due in money may be very great. On the other hand, when prices are advancing, the gross profit is less than the interest, because the value of the principal, when it is returned, will be less. Interest is only equivalent to profit in cases where prices remain uniform during the life of the loan. When prices are declining, therefore, the borrowing producer will be willing to pay a very small interest, because he expects to be obliged to repay to the lender a greater value than he received from him, and the lender will be willing to receive a very small rate, as he expects to receive in repayment a greater value than he parted with. But, if he expects prices to decline, a mere speculator will not pay even a small rate of interest, because in such case, as he is not a producer, there will be no profit at all for it to be subtracted from, but a loss to be added to the interest he pays. We see, therefore, that it is utterly impossible for a large accumulation of wealth of itself to lead to any speculation. If prices have, indeed, declined too far, some advance in them may be looked for, but, as long as stocks continue large, every one knows that it can be but a moderate one, and no great speculation can ensue. That is a luxury that the community only indulges in when there is apprehension of a scarcity. Mill's explanation of panics, as due to the speculation engendered by a low rate of profit and the accumulation of capital for which no legitimate avenues of investment are open, is not only inadequate, but diametrically opposed to what really occurs. When commodities are scarce, speculation really sets in. There are always in the community shrewd individuals who perceive that a scarcity is imminent, and buy for a rise before prices are affected, or fully affected, and they are the better enabled to do this because, their speculations being more or less closely confined to the commodities in which they are accustomed to deal, they have better means of information than others as to the quantity of them in existence. It will soon be found, however, after a period of low profits and prices, that other articles are also scarce, and speculation will become more and more general, and prices will advance all along the line.

But such speculative purchases will not at all affect the proportional amount of loanable funds to the demand for them, though they will very much increase the number of exchanges of property and the number of discounts that will be called for. They have a powerful effect in increasing the amount of productive consumption, as they relieve the producing classes of the dead stock they were carrying, and supply them with money or the right to demand money, from which alone the wages-fund can be supplied. Before they were so relieved, the producers were forced into the loan market, pledging their goods to avoid the necessity of overpressing the sales of their dead stock. The speculators merely take their place as borrowers, and do not even increase the activity of the loan market, except as they purchase and repurchase of each other.

When the crisis has come and prices begin to tumble, the high rate of interest likewise is no proof of the scarcity of loanable funds in proportion to the demand. It is caused by the greater supposed risk then incurred in lending, and the anxiety of bankers to retain more than their proportion of the reserve, and is really somewhat mitigated by the expectation of a decline in general prices.

What, then, does determine the average rate of interest? We may answer that it will be such percentage of the principal as, together with an addition for any expected fall, or with a subtraction for any expected rise in general prices, will equal the average rate of profit of other capital similarly circumstanced as to risk, trouble, and skill. While the average rates of interest and profit bear a constant ratio to each other, the rates that prevail at any particular time do not do so, but may vary almost indefinitely, and the one affords but a slight indication of what the other is. The only law that we can affirm is, that during dull times the rate of interest tends to be lower than the rate of profit, and during good times, when prices are advancing, higher, except as affected by the risk involved.

To illustrate our meaning, which is, perhaps, as yet obscure to the reader, let us suppose five capitalists—M, B, W, R, and F—whom we will consider to represent five separate classes, and to constitute, with the laborers, a community by themselves. Let M be a manufacturer; B, a banker; W, a wholesaler or jobber; R, a retailer; and F, a farmer. Let us further suppose them all to be possessed of an equal amount of circulating capital: M's will consist of manufactured foods and F's of raw products and food, while W's and R's will be composed partly of goods and partly of food and raw products, and B's will be money.

Now, in a state of barter, M and F would exchange with each other directly, or indirectly through W and R, and B's capital would lie idle. Under a cash system, B's capital would come into play. He would, at first, be the only purchaser, and would buy, as the humor took him, indifferently from the other four; but he could only purchase for unproductive consumption, and would finally be eliminated from the problem. Under the credit system, he would, however, be able to obtain a profit for his capital. M and F are both desirous of disposing of their stock, but neither wants the goods of the other, nor those of W and R. What they do want is money with which to pay wages and continue their productive consumption. W and R desire to dispose of their goods and buy those of M and F, but can not do so unless they can get the money. W, therefore, goes to B, and pledges his capital for money, with which he buys M's goods, who immediately deposits the money with B, or W gives M his note for his goods, which B discounts for M, who pays it out in wages, and the laborers expend the same sum with R, who deposits it with B; or if M's goods do not suit W, or if M prefers to hold them, M goes direct to B and obtains the money he needs for wages by pledging his goods to him, and this money soon returns to B through R or W or F. Now we will suppose W desirous of also buying F's goods. He can do as he did with M, for B has the whole of his original capital to lend him, and he can give security upon the goods that formerly belonged to M. Now we will suppose a second M and a second F, with like capital and goods to the first, and W is still able to buy their goods, because B is still able to lend him the funds. However great the increase of M's and F's, the original W's, R's, and B's could take care of their trade, provided no change in prices occurred, and the money withdrawn by one party were immediately returned to B by another; and, if we suppose B to possess enough more capital than the others to provide for such contingencies, the last condition can be eliminated. Now, if by increase of loanable funds Mill means an increase of gold or other money, he is undoubtedly wrong in affirming that the rate of interest would be lowered. B, not being able at first to loan all his capital, might for a time lower his profits to induce the others to borrow more, but very shortly the value of their goods would rise, and B could then employ both his new and his old money at the previous rate. But if Mill means the general increase of the wealth of the community, such increase does not, under the conditions we have supposed, at all affect the demand and supply of loanable funds. If we suppose them doubled all round, or some of them doubled, some not, the ratio would be the same, and, if the rate of interest truly depended upon such ratio, it would always be uniform.

But, although the demand and supply of loanable funds can not vary except together, the activity of the money market may vary, just as the activity of exchange may, although the demand and supply of commodities are equivalent terms, and the activity of the one as of the other will vary from the same cause, viz., the increase or decrease of profits.

In our illustration we have supposed prices of everything, labor included, to remain uniform. Now, let us see how our five capitalists would act when prices did vary. If all prices, including the price of labor, varied together, as soon as exportation or importation had adjusted the amount of gold thereto, the old conditions would be restored: let us suppose the prices of commodities fall, and the price of labor does not fall, or, what is the same thing, that labor rises in money price, while commodities remain stationary or fall. It is evident that M and F will borrow more than they did if they go on producing; but they will be under no necessity of borrowing of B at all, supposing their stock not to be in excess of their capital and they totally cease producing. Let us suppose that they go on producing, but only to half the former extent; all the exchanges we have supposed will go on exactly as they did before, but they will only be to about half the amount. B's capital, as before, would remain in his hands, and the ratio of deposits to discounts would remain nearly the same as it previously was, and they alone constitute the demand and supply of the loan market. B's capital, which, by supposition, consists wholly of money, if the system of payment is entirely by checking, will never be out of his hands, and is in no sense an addition to loanable funds, but purely and simply an instrument of exchange, and could be entirely dispensed with without any effect upon the loan market, if it were not needed as an element of confidence.

The cause of money being tight or plenty is that our system of banking is not ideally perfect. If it were so, no activity in the loan market would have the slightest effect upon bankers' reserves; as it is, more is required when the sum total of discounts is large, to allow for the transfer of funds, and this amount comes, of course, from the reserve. Now, it is only as this reserve is affected that lenders will be able to exact more, or be willing to take less, than such rate of interest as will yield them the average rate of profit at the time, consideration being, of course, given to risk, trouble, and skill, and to the expectation of a rise or decline in the exchange value of money. Under an ideally perfect system of banking, by which we mean that all transfers were by check alone, bankers would be wholly unable to affect the total reserve; and, as it is, they have very limited power of doing it. But individual bankers can decrease or increase their own reserve, though at the expense of the reserves of others, and the disposition during dull times to lend a portion of it, and during times of activity when the reserve diminishes, or of panic when each banker desires to accumulate in his vaults all he can, irrespective of any profit he may thereby fail to obtain, the eagerness to retain the utmost share of the total reserve, enables bankers to fix the rate of interest below or above what may be called the normal rate. The interest of money is, therefore, affected by the activity of the loan market, but in no sense depends upon the ratio of demand and supply of loanable funds. Anything which affects the proportion between money and other commodities affects likewise the rate of interest, but only until prices are adjusted to the new conditions. Great speculators frequently avail themselves of this, and temporarily raise the rate of interest by locking up large amounts of money; if, however, they should permanently abstract such funds from the circulation, the rate of interest, other things remaining the same, would be the same as before, as soon as prices had sufficiently fallen.

Through one circumstance, however, the increase of loans does affect the rate of interest. We have seen that the rate is raised by any decrease in the reserve of bankers. Such reserve is needed as an element of confidence and to allow of the fluctuations in the amount of the individual reserves of professional lenders. We have also seen that, when the loan market is active, the total reserve will be decreased on account of the greater amount of money in transit; but in addition to this the proportion between the reserve and the amount of loans is disturbed by an increase of the amount on loan. This, so far as it occurs, impairs confidence and adds somewhat to the risk of lending. The only influence which causes the rate of interest to differ from the rate of profit is the expectation that prices will decline or rise during the life of the loan, as the difference in the nominal rates caused by want of confidence is at bottom caused by the risk or supposed risk involved, and this is always considered and defined as an element of the rate of profit itself.

Mill's apprehension of the phenomena of the loan market seems to me to be open to the same objections, which he derives from Say, and opposes to the idea that the supply of commodities does not itself constitute the demand for commodities. I have here criticised his views, not because they have any effect upon the main theme of this treatise—the relation of capital to population—but because he attempts to find in them the sole causes of commercial crises and industrial stagnation, the comprehension of which is only possible when such relations are clearly understood. The idea that the rate of interest depends upon the demand and supply of loanable funds or upon the amount actually on loan at the time, is certainly misleading; that rate is entirely governed by the element of the supposed risk involved, and the exchangeable value of the use of capital at the time; and it is only as influencing these two elements that the activity or amount of loans has any effect.

CHAPTER VII.

WAGES AND PROFITS.

It were a desideratum in economic discussion that the word "wages" should never be used without a prefix. The subjects, in discussing which the term comes into play, are so complicated that no mind is able to carry its connotations without occasionally tripping, when the unqualified term is alike used for its three very distinct significations, which I would distinguish as *proportional*, *real*, and *money* wages.

The word "proportional" is my own, and will not be met with elsewhere, at least to my knowledge. I have so far used it without explanation, as my meaning was sufficiently distinct for the previous stages of the argument. Mill and Ricardo express the idea by the generic term "wages" alone, and especially note the fact in each instance, when they desire to distinguish it from real or money wages. I can not but think that this has led them into some confusion, and prevented them from perceiving several of the implications of their argument. I must confess I am unable in places to understand exactly what they mean by "wages," and to such extent, that I find it difficult to criticise their doctrines before defining what I understand and mean to express by the three terms "proportional, real, and money wages."

Proportional wages, then, I understand, or, rather as the term is my own, I define to be, the proportion of the product received as wages by the laborer or laborers who produced it, after a deduction from such product is made for rent and for the profits of any fixed capital employed. If any material enter into the product not produced by the laborers, whose proportional wages are under consideration, its cost and the profit thereon are also to be first deducted. After rent, raw produce, and the use of fixed capital are paid for, the proportion in which what remains is divided between the laborers and the owners of the active stock determines this rate of wages and the rate of profit. It is not, as might at first be supposed, as owners of dead stock also that the share of capitalists must be computed; the motive of their engaging in production includes, indeed, the profit on dead as well as on active stock. If the rate of profit on the entire capital expended as wages, and in holding their goods for a market, is insufficient, they will not produce. But the profit on dead stock must here be considered as equivalent to a profit on fixed capital, and as not affecting the computation of the rate of proportional wages. To illustrate, we will suppose two capitalists, one of whom produces wheat and the other wine, and that the wheat can be sold within the year, while the wine can not find a market under two years. It is clear that the larger profits of the wine-grower should not be considered as lowering the proportional wages of his employés or the *rate* of profit he obtains. During the last year it is kept, the wine may be fairly considered, for the purposes of this discussion, as fixed, not circulating capital. The proportion of the product which goes to capital varies, of course, according to the amount of capital employed, as well as with the rate of profit obtained. What determines the rate of wages, however, is not the amount, but simply the rate of profit. We do not mean, therefore, by "proportional" that the proportion is between the wages-fund and the gross product. Such proportion can vary indefinitely as machinery is substituted for manual exertion, or as the normal amount of dead stock is increased without disturbing the "cost of labor" to the capitalist, or the reward of labor to his employés. But, while not affecting the computation of the rate of proportional wages, the amount of profit on fixed capital and dead stock profoundly affects the tendency to a rise or fall of such wages? Capitalists do not ordinarily distinguish in their calculations between such profits and those they receive on their expenditure for wages, nor, indeed, need they, as they never vary in their comparative rate to any appreciable amount. If the general rate of profit is low, proportional wages will be high, with a tendency to decrease; if it is high, such wages will be low, with a tendency to increase.

The amount of dead stock in existence does, however —proportional wages remaining the same—considerably affect real wages, when such dead stock is partly composed of things that laborers are accustomed to consume. The rate of profit remaining the same, the larger the amount of such things in existence, the higher will be the price in proportion to the money-wages that the laborer must pay for them, and the smaller the amount of such things he is able to consume. The laborer's interests are, therefore, subserved by any policy or event which decreases the normal amount of dead stock, at least so far as it consists of articles he consumes.

It is customary for economists to assert indifferently

that the rate of wages depends on the ratio of capital to population, and on the demand and supply of labor. They consider the two to be equivalent propositions. If they mean, as the exigencies of their argument demand, proportional wages, they are right as to the former, but wrong as to the latter proposition, and the two propositions are the opposite of equivalent. When the ratio of capital to population is the largest, is exactly the time when the demand for labor is the least. The demand does not depend upon the amount of commodities physically available for the wages fund, but upon the amount that can be employed with a profit as active stock. This amount, we have seen, varies inversely with the amount of circulating capital in gross, and we have the apparent anomaly that the exchangeable value of labor, unlike that of other commodities, is highest when the demand for it is least, the supply remaining, by supposition, the same. The explanation lies in the fact, that such a state of affairs depresses the exchangeable value of the commodities in which wages are really paid, more than it depresses the exchangeable value of labor, and, value being a relative term, the value of labor as compared with such commodities is enhanced. If any commodity be an exception to the increase of the ratio of capital to population, the exchangeable value of both labor and the other commodities (food, clothing, etc.), in which labor is really paid, will fall as compared with it. If they fall equally and the commodity be gold, the money rate of wages will decline, but not the proportional rate. When any material commodity is relatively in excess, its exchangeable value is lessened, because the commodities with which it exchanges are not relatively superabundant. But when the supply of labor exceeds the demand it does so only because the supply of the things for which it is exchangeable are in excess to a greater degree. Its exchangeable value, therefore, can not be decreased, but must be enhanced by any decrease in the demand for labor coincident with and caused by an increase in the ratio of capital to population.

The rate of wages does not depend upon the demand for labor, but the demand depends upon it. The tendency to a rise or fall of the rate does indeed depend upon the extent of the demand, but such influence can only become operative when the demand has first changed, by its effect upon production and accumulation, the ratio of capital to population. What does directly depend upon the demand for labor is the amount of employment, the number of laborers that can be kept at work; while the rate of proportional wages depends solely on the ratio of capital to population.

The efficiency of labor has nothing to do with the rate of proportional wages, nor has the margin of cultivation. Proportional wages are equal whenever the rate of profit is the same, whether or not it takes in one place one hundred laborers to produce the same amount of commodities that fifty produce elsewhere. Neither has the price of labor anything to do with the rate. A rise in real or money wages may or may not be a rise in proportional, but a rise in proportional, or in money wages, other things remaining the same, necessarily entails a fall in real wages, as we shall now see in proceeding to a consideration of the latter.

The rate of real wages can be ascertained by dividing the amount of the wages-fund by the whole number of laborers, not by the number only of those employed. The latter division would ascertain for us what is popularly called the "going" rate of wages, and that name for them will do as well as any other, as what such rate is does not much affect the principles or deductions of the science. In defining real wages, Mill says, in Book II, chapter xxvi, section 1:

"What is here meant, however, by wages, is the laborer's real scale of comfort; the quantity he obtains of the things which nature or habit has made necessary or agreeable to him; wages, in the sense in which they are of importance to the receiver."

And in the preceding paragraph he affirms that such

"wages depend on the ratio between population and capital; and would do so if all the capital in the world were the property of one association, or if the capitalists among whom it is shared maintained each an establishment for the production of every article consumed in the community, exchange of commodities having no existence. As the ratio between capital and population, in all old countries, depends on the strength of the checks by which the too rapid increase of population is restrained, it may be said, popularly speaking, that wages depend on the checks to population; that when the check is not death, by starvation or disease, wages depend on the prudence of the laboring people; and that wages in any country are habitually at the lowest rate to which in that country the laborer will suffer them to be depressed rather than put a restraint upon multiplication."

This definition I accept: the affirmation I have repeatedly shown to be true inversely, and in a sense directly the reverse of Mill's.

Other things being equal, the rate of real and proportional wages varies inversely, though not in strict proportion. A rise in the latter always entails a loss of employment, which usually more than offsets to the laborer the benefit of the rise: a rise of two per cent would probably be followed by a decrease of ten or twenty per cent in the number of laborers employed. (I am speaking now of the temporary rise that occurs periodically in the fluctuations of trade, and not of the decrease in what may be called the normal rate of profit that proceeds with the growth and civilization of a country. This decline of the normal rate does not lead to any cessation of industry. Capitalists, being as well satisfied with the smaller rate as they were before with the larger, are equally willing to employ their funds productively.) There is no necessary ratio between the rise in proportional and the fall in real wages. Such rise may entail a slight and lasting or a severe and transient cessation of employment, which, when it occurs, will depend upon various causes, many of which may be accidental, and not due to the action of economic law; unless, however, the economic conditions are disturbed by abnormal causes, such, for instance, as the occurrence of war, the detriment to the laborer through the decrease of employment must be many times the advantage gained by the rise of his proportional wages. It must be so by about the amount that productive consumption is decreased during the period of lessened production.

Although, in his main argument, Mill constantly affirms that "wages" and the rate of profit vary inversely, he qualifies the statement, in the succeeding quotation from him, by substituting the term "cost of labor" for "wages":

"We thus arrive at the conclusion of Ricardo and others, that the rate of profits depends on wages; rising as wages fall, and falling as wages rise. In adopting, however, this doctrine, I must insist upon making a most necessary alteration in its wording. Instead of saying that profits depend on wages, let us say (what Ricardo really meant) that they depend on the cost of labor.

"Wages and the cost of labor—what labor brings in to the laborer, and what it costs to the capitalists—are ideas quite distinct, and which it is of the utmost importance to keep so. For this purpose it is essential not to designate them, as is almost always done, by the same name. Wages in public discussions, both oral and printed, being looked upon from the point of view of the payers, much oftener than from that of the receivers, nothing is more common than to say that wages are high or low, meaning only that the cost of labor is high or low. The reverse of this would be oftener the truth; the cost of labor is frequently at its highest where wages are lowest. This may arise from two causes. In the first place, the labor, though cheap, may be inefficient. In no European country are wages so low as they are (or, at least, were) in Ireland; the remuneration of an agricultural laborer in the west of Ireland not being more than half the wages of even the lowest-paid Englishman, the Dorsetshire laborer. But if, from inferior skill and industry, two days' labor of an Irishman accomplished no more work than an English laborer performed in one, the Irishman's labor cost as much as the Englishman's, though it brought in so much less to himself. The capitalist's profit is determined by the former of these two things, not by the latter. That a difference to this extent really existed in the efficiency of the labor, is proved not only by abundant testimony, but by the fact that, notwithstanding the lowness of wages, profits of capital are not understood to have been higher in Ireland than in England.

"The other cause which renders wages and the cost of labor no real criteria of one another is the varying costliness of the articles which the laborer consumes. If these are cheap, wages, in the sense which is of importance to the laborer, may be high, and yet the cost of labor may be low; if dear, the laborer may be wretchedly off, though his labor may cost much to the capitalist. This last is the condition of a country overpeopled in relation to its land; in which, food being dear, the poorness of the laborer's real reward does not prevent labor from costing much to the purchaser, and low wages and low profits coexist. The opposite case is exemplified in the United States of America. The laborer there enjoys a greater abundance of comforts than in any other country of the world, except some of the newest colonies; but, owing to the cheap price at which these comforts can be obtained (combined with the great efficiency of the labor), the cost of labor is, at least, not higher, nor the rate of profit lower, than in Europe.

"The cost of labor, then, is, in the language of mathematics, a function of three variables: the efficiency of labor; the wages of labor (meaning thereby the real reward of the laborer); and the greater or less cost at which the articles composing that real reward can be produced or procured. It is plain that the cost of labor to the capitalist must be influenced by each of these three circumstances, and by no others. These, therefore, are also the circumstances which determine the rate of profit; and it can not be in any way affected, except through one or the other of them. If labor generally became more efficient, without being more highly rewarded; if, without its becoming less efficient, its remuneration fell, no increase taking place in the cost of the articles composing that remuneration; or, if those articles became less costly, without the laborer's obtaining more of them—in any one of these three cases, profits would rise. If, on the contrary, labor became less efficient (as it might do from diminished bodily vigor in the people, destruction of fixed capital, or deteriorated education); or, if the laborer obtained a higher remuneration, without any increased cheapness in the things composing it; or if, without his obtaining more, that which he did obtain became more costly—profits, in all these cases, would suffer a diminution. And there is no other combination of circumstances in which the general rate of profit of a country, in all employments indifferently, can either fall or rise."—(Mill, Book II, chapter xv, section 7.)

The proportion between real and proportional wages, besides the effect of their tendency to vary inversely, is also affected by the margin of cultivation; the physical efficiency of the laborers—their education or mental efficiency—any social custom, or other cause, which prevents a part of their number from finding employment, and the degree of skill demanded by the nature of the national industries.

As, in the quotation above, Mill and Ricardo uniformly assume that real and proportional wages only differ from the first three of these causes, the latter two they seem to have overlooked, while they certainly, by implication, deny what I have endeavored to establish as the greatest difference between them—the tendency to vary inversely through the effect upon the amount of employment of a rise or fall of the rate of profit. This last cause of difference has received enough of our attention, and nothing in this connection calls for any further remarks upon the effect of the margin of cultivation, or of the physical or mental efficiency of the laborers, except to notice in passing, that the margin of cultivation is by far the most important determinant of the rate of real wages; the other two remaining causes are, however, of great moment, especially as affecting subjects to be hereafter considered, and because they have so generally been ignored.

I would remark, then, that anything which prevents those debarred, by physical or mental disability, or by sex, from seeking or finding general employment, from seeking or finding the special employment, for which they are fitted, lowers the rate of real wages as compared with proportional, and is a deduction from the comforts and subsistence of the laboring classes, exactly equal to what such persons would earn if employed, or rather to what those whose places they took would earn if employed, as they would necessarily very soon be, since the increase in the number of laborers, involved in such change of employment, could not but affect favorably the rate of profit, and correspondingly enlarge the demand for labor. But that they should be engaged productively is likewise to the advantage of the capitalist, because it increases the normal ratio which capital can bear to population without increasing the population itself. The additional production that would then take place would allow of further accumulation by the rich, sufficient to employ such labor, without lowering the rate of profit at all. It is the interest of employer and employé alike that all their fellow-citizens should be engaged productively. We suffer, perhaps, from no greater economic evil than the social custom which discourages one half the human family—the female sex—from engaging in productive employment, and condemns them almost entirely to unproductive services, or an idle dependence upon producers, as a means of support. Nature has, indeed, apportioned the household duties to the wives, mothers, and daughters, and these duties are necessarily of the nature of services, and not productive; but the demand for these services does not happen to be sufficient to employ the whole or nearly the whole sex, and the labor of those not needed should be productively engaged. If it were, it is not too much to assert that the annual produce of the country would be increased at least ten to fifteen per cent, and such increase would be a pure addition to net as well as gross income. But another economic effect would follow of incalculable importance to the future of the race. The tendency of population to press upon the food-supply would certainly be lessened and probably obliterated by it. The great addition to income involved would not only be mainly devoted to a rise in the standard of living, but the opportunity of self-support would remove the necessity of matrimony to women as the only alternative by which they can hope to escape starvation or dependence. Besides which, marriage between young men and women, productively employed, would involve a positive decrease of their joint income, that could not fail of acting as a preventive to unwise unions. Political economy has been named "the dismal science," for no other reason than the seeming impossibility of applying really efficient preventive checks to the too rapid increase of population, that are not also subversive of the best social instincts of the race. But here is a check probably of itself sufficient, that will accord with and not antagonize personal inclination.

If, then, the proper aim of government is the good of the whole, women have a right to claim, while debarred by social custom from other employments, the exclusive appointment to every office the duties of which are not inconsistent with their physical organization or moral delicacy, even in cases where their efficiency is so inferior to that of men as to involve a considerable additional expense to the government. Such a national policy, once established, would also encourage the employment of female labor by private individuals, with the effect of considerably increasing the national prosperity.

But the policy of government providing a stimulus to the employment of female labor also affects the question of free trade and protection. Most of our protected industries, especially the manufacture of textile fabrics, employ large numbers of women and girls, who would not otherwise be productively employed at all in the agricultural or household pursuits from which our protective policy has diverted them. The value of this labor —and it is certainly not less than fifty per cent of that employed in our cotton, woolen, and silk mills—is to be offset against any loss in the efficiency of our labor from what it would have been under free trade, before any decrease in the productive capacity of the nation can be attributed to protection.

The following passage from Mill, in a note to Book I,

chapter v, section 1, fully sustains in principle the position here taken:

> "An exception must be admitted when the industry created or upheld by the restrictive law belongs to the class of what are called domestic manufactures. These being carried on by persons *already fed*—by laboring families, in the intervals of other employment—no transfer of capital to the occupation is necessary to its being undertaken, beyond the value of the materials and tools, which is often inconsiderable. If, therefore, a protecting duty causes this occupation to be carried on, when it otherwise would not, there is in this case a real increase of the production of the country."

This leads us to make the same remark of the remaining cause of difference between real and proportional wages. Any increase of skill required of the laborer, by a change in the nature of his trade, is a direct benefit to the laboring classes, as it raises some of their number to a higher social status, in which they are able to raise the average rate of real, without any increase of proportional, wages. The skill required of artisans and the rate of real wages that they receive are on the average, in every land, decidedly greater than the skill demanded of and the real wages accorded to agricultural laborers. Whatever this addition to real wages, due to protection, may be, it is also to be offset against any losses due to the same cause. The gain is considerable, but not equal to that of the employment of female labor. It may, perhaps, be estimated at from ten to fifteen per cent of the male labor diverted from agriculture to manufactures.

It is important to notice that both these gains, whatever they are, accrue mainly to the benefit of labor, and do not add to the rate of profits, or to its gross amount, except as they allow of more capital being accumulated and profitably employed, and that they find no expression in the prices at which international exchanges take place. If, in all countries, journeymen watch-makers earned in a day five times as much as common laborers, and it took ten days' labor to make a watch, a country, in which the margin of cultivation was such that the wages of common labor was one dollar per day, could produce a watch for fifty dollars, while a more fertile and less peopled land, where labor was worth one dollar and a half per day, could not produce the watch under seventy-five dollars. Under free trade, the latter would buy watches of its less fertile and overpeopled neighbor, and would apparently save twenty-five dollars on each watch by so doing; whereas the apparent gain of its neighbor would be only five dollars, that being by supposition the difference between the productive efficiency of ten days' agricultural labor in the respective countries. Supposing the efficiency of artisan labor to be the same in each country, the joint gain of the interchange would only be that resulting from the fertile soil of the one being cultivated in place of the more sterile soil of the other. This gain amounts to five dollars, and is the identical five dollars gained by the watch-making nation; whereas the twenty-five-dollar gain to the agricultural nation is only apparent, being under protection a mere transfer from the consumer to the skilled artisan.

By diverting ten days' labor from agriculture to the better-paid watch-making, the over-populated country has gained a value of forty dollars. By a like diversion, which could, however, only take place under protection, the under-populated country would increase the value of its products to the extent of sixty dollars; twenty-five of them, however, being at the expense of its own consumers, its net gain would be only thirty-five. In such case protection would result in a loss to the world of five dollars, but also to such a redistribution of wealth as would result in a net gain to the protected country of thirty-five dollars, and a net loss to its manufacturing neighbor of forty. In my illustration, I have supposed that the ratio of skilled to common wages was the same in both places. This, however, except for convenience of calculation, makes no difference, as long as, in both places, there is some distinction made in favor of skilled labor. The expense of educating the laborers to their higher condition of life is also, of course, to be deducted from the net gain of thirty-five dollars.*

* "Although, however, general wages, whether high or low, do not affect values, yet if wages are higher in one employment than another, or if they rise or fall permanently in one employment without doing so in others, these inequalities do really operate upon values. The causes which make wages vary from one employment to another have been considered in a former chapter. When the wages of an employment permanently exceed the average rate, the value of the thing produced will, in the same degree, exceed the standard determined by mere quantity of labor. Things, for example, which are made by skilled labor, exchange for the produce of a much greater quantity of unskilled labor; for no reason but because the labor is more highly paid. If, through the extension of education, the laborers competent to skilled employments were so increased in number as to diminish the difference between their wages and those of common labor, all things produced by labor of the superior kind would fall in value, compared with things produced by common labor, and these might be said, therefore, to rise in value. We have before remarked that the difficulty of passing from one class of employments to a class greatly superior has hitherto caused the wages of all those classes of laborers who are separated from one another by any very marked barrier to depend more than might be supposed upon the increase of the population of each class, considered separately; and that the inequalities in the remuneration of labor are much greater than could exist if the competition of the laboring people generally could be brought practically to bear on each particular employment.

"It thus appears that the maxim laid down by some of the best political economists, that wages do not enter into value, is expressed with greater

The consideration of money-wages need not detain us long. Their rate is evidently ascertained by dividing the money value of the wages-fund by the number of laborers employed. That of real wages is determined by the ratio of the utility of the wages-fund to the whole number of laborers, while the rate of proportional wages is, strictly speaking, not a rate of wages at all, but is the ratio of the wages-fund itself to the gross product after rental and the use of fixed capital are paid for. The consideration of money-wages is chiefly of interest, because it is through change in them that changes in the others are effected. It is at present sufficient for my purpose to say that a general rise in money-wages, other money values remaining the same, or, in other words, a

latitude than the truth warrants, or than accords with their own meaning. Wages do enter into value. The relative wages of the labor necessary for producing different commodities affect their value just as much as the relative quantities of labor. It is true, the absolute wages paid have no effect upon values; but neither has the absolute quantity of labor. If that were to vary simultaneously and equally in all commodities, values would not be affected. If, for instance, the general efficiency of all labor were increased, so that all things without exception could be produced in the same quantity as before with a smaller amount of labor, no trace of this general diminution of cost of production would show itself in the values of commodities. Any change which might take place in them would only represent the unequal degrees in which the improvement affected different things; and would consist in cheapening those in which the saving of labor had been the greatest, while those in which there had been some, but a less saving of labor, would actually rise in value. In strictness, therefore, wages of labor have as much to do with value as quantity of labor; and neither Ricardo nor any one else has denied the fact. In considering, however, the causes of variation in value, quantity of labor is the thing of chief importance; for, when that varies, it is generally in one or a few commodities at a time, but the variations of wages (except passing fluctuations) are usually general, and have no considerable effect on value."—(Mill, Book III, chapter iv, section 3.)

relative rise, results always in a rise of proportional and a fall in real wages, through cessation of employment.

It may be well, in closing this chapter, to remark that the result of the discussion as to whether such a fund as the wages-fund really exists will not affect the argument. All that is implied by the term, as I have used it, could have been as well expressed by the term "gross amount of wages." To my mind, it seems evident that past and present social and economic conditions do accurately predetermine the amount that will be expended in wages, to such degree that the amount of that fund may be strictly considered as set apart; but, if by predetermination it is meant that the amount of the wages-fund is predetermined by the intentions of capitalists, I do not view it as governed by such intentions, except to a very slight and temporary amount.

CHAPTER VIII.

CAPITAL AND LABOR.

The consideration that we have just given to wages will enable us to appreciate better the true relations of capital and labor.

The interest of the laborer lies solely in the rate of his real wages, and any change in proportional or in money wages is a matter of indifference to him, except as such change affects the rate of real. The sole interest of the capitalist, however, is that the rate of proportional wages should be low, and he has no economic concern with real or money wages, except as they affect proportional.

It has been commonly assumed that, while capitalists and laborers were both interested that the gross annual produce should be as large as possible, their interests were antagonistic when it came to a division of the spoils, and that any increase in the share of one class could only be at the expense of a decrease, not only of the relative but of the absolute share of the other. Now, this is true as far as individuals actually engaged in production divide a certain fixed product, but not true of the absolute share of either class as a whole, because there is a division of present products that by leading to an increase of future products increases the absolute share of each class, though not, of course, the relative share of one or the other of them. It can not, indeed, be asserted that the points at which the absolute share of each will be the greatest always coincide exactly, but the points are evidently very near together—so near, that the attainment of one will practically be the attainment of the other also.

In any given society, it is the interest of the capitalists that capital should bear such a ratio to population, as that the sum arrived at by multiplying the gross capital by the rate of profit, which normally results from such ratio, shall be the greatest. Any increase of capital, beyond that amount, will augment the gross sum on which profit is attained, but lessen the rate—any decrease will augment the rate, and lessen the gross sum; but in either event the gross income derived from profits will be decreased. The interest of the laborer will likewise be subserved when capital bears such a ratio to population that the sum arrived at by multiplying the number of laborers employed by the average rate of their proportional wages, or, in other words, the total wages-fund, shall be the greatest. Any increase of capital, beyond that amount, will augment the rate, but decrease the number employed; and any decrease will augment the number, but decrease the rate; and in either event the gross income from wages will be lessened. The interests of both classes are therefore identical in the increase of the gross product, and very nearly, if not quite, identical in its division also, because the ratio of capital to population ultimately depends upon such division.

But, as I have before remarked, the interests of individuals do not coincide with the interests of the classes to which they belong. Every employer will grow richer by paying low wages, and every laborer by exacting high ones, at least as compared with their fellow employers and employés. We have here a case in which individual are opposed to social interests. The antagonism between labor and capital results wholly from the growth of class out of individual animosities. It subserves the interest of every employer that other capitalists should pay higher wages than he does, and the interest of every laborer that other laborers should work for lower wages than his own. The individual interest of each is really coincident with that of the class to which he does not belong. When this is recognized, and not before, may we expect the two classes to harmonize in their feelings and actions.

While the ratio of capital to population that yields the greatest income to capital may not always be identical with that which yields the greatest income to labor, it is evident that the ratio which leads to the greatest annual production subserves best the interest of the community, and that political and social action should, as far as possible, be directed to secure such ratio, with a leaning, perhaps, to the interests of labor from humane but not from economic motives.

The real interest of the laboring classes is in real wages, and this interest can be advanced: First, by increasing their own efficiency by a more faithful and industrious performance of their duties. As they receive much the greater part of the gross produce, they themselves suffer the greater part of the loss resulting from laziness and inefficiency. The immediate loss, indeed, falls upon their employers, but they distribute this among the consumers of their goods by enhancing their price, and the laborers themselves suffer it ultimately as such consumers. Secondly, by any change in the nature of the national industries, by which more of the class are raised from the position of common laborers to that of skilled artisans. Thirdly, by increasing the proportion of their own number who enter the labor market as competitors for employment. I refer here chiefly to the employment to a greater extent of female labor. Fourthly and lastly, by never seeking to raise their proportional wages to a point that will allow capital such scant remuneration as will lead to a decline of production.

Owing to the conflict between individual and social or class interests, to which I have already adverted, the class action of laborers, as it has expressed itself in trades-unions, has been diametrically opposed to their true interests as here ascertained. First, they have endeavored to lessen their own efficiency in production. Secondly, their action has tended to discourage any change in the nature of industry in the direction of substituting skilled for common labor, because it is in skilled industries alone that they are able to combine effectually enough to influence at all the rate of profit and the expense of conducting such industries; besides which, in such industries, by enforcing the occasional idleness of fixed capital, they augment in them the amount of capital that is necessary, and thus lessen not only the absolute but the relative share of the produce that accrues to themselves. Thirdly, they have failed to demand, as their moral and political right, the greater employment of female and prison labor; and, fourthly, they have persistently endeavored to raise the rate of proportional wages beyond the point that allowed of such a rate of profit as was consistent with the highest rate of real wages.

Their whole action has been directed, not only toward

the lessening of the gross sum, of which they obtain a part, but to the reduction against themselves of the ratio in which that sum is divided between capital and labor. They have succeeded in reducing, not only their absolute but in some degree their relative share; for this mistaken action they can not be blamed, if real and proportional wages coincide to the degree taught by English economists, and if over-accumulation is really not antagonistic to their employment in production. If I am wrong, their action is, in the main, right, and little improvement in their condition can be hoped for; but, if I am correct, it lies in the power of the laboring classes to nearly or quite double their real, without increasing in the least the rate of their proportional wages. The truer perception of the real relations of capital and labor, acquired by the recognition of the constant tendency of capital to press upon population, affords the only solution of the labor question, with its resulting problems of socialism and revolution. The condition of our laboring classes is very unsatisfactory, and daily becoming more so, "where wealth accumulates and men decay." They have a right to demand such social reorganization as shall give them a far greater absolute, though not relative, share of the earth's products than they now receive; and that this can, in a measure, be done, not only not to the detriment, but to the positive advantage of capital, I have certainly made evident.

I must confess myself somewhat surprised at the following passage from Mill's work, Book V, chapter x, section 5:

"If it were possible for the working classes, by combining among themselves, to raise or keep up the general rate of wages, it need hardly be said that this would be a thing not to be punished, but to be welcomed and rejoiced at. Unfortunately, the effect is quite beyond attainment by such means. The multitudes who compose the working class are too numerous and too widely scattered to combine at all, much more to combine effectually. If they could do so, they might doubtless succeed in diminishing the hours of labor, and obtaining the same wages for less work. But if they aim at obtaining actually higher wages than the rate fixed by demand and supply—the rate which distributes the whole circulating capital of the country among the entire working population—this could only be accomplished by keeping a part of their number permanently out of employment. As support from public charity would of course be refused to those who could get work and would not accept it, they would be thrown for support upon the trades-union of which they were members; and the work-people, collectively, would be no better off than before, having to support the same numbers out of the same aggregate wages. In this way, however, the class would have its attention forcibly drawn to the effect of a superfluity of numbers, and to the necessity, if they would have high wages, of proportioning the supply of labor to the demand."

No passage more fertile than this in economic errors was ever penned, and an analysis of it will therefore serve admirably to exemplify the difference between Mill's views and my own.

If, by combining, he means to assert that the laborers might be able to retain the same rate of proportional wages while shortening the hours of labor, I reply that, while this is technically true, it is not true in the sense that Mill intends. Even if the proportion between the number of laborers employed and the amount of the wages-fund might be maintained, the employment of a relatively larger active fixed capital would be necessary—the same amount of buildings, tools, and machinery being required for short as for long hours; but such proportion would not be maintained, on account of the fall in profits. Labor, therefore, would receive a relatively smaller share of a relatively smaller produce, unless, indeed, more work was accomplished in the short than in the long hours. Such a combination, if successful, could not fail to greatly depress the rate of real wages as compared with proportional, and is reprehensible in its effects upon both labor and capital, and especially so in its effect upon the laborers themselves, though it is not a proper subject for legislative repression. Mill here affirms by implication that real and proportional wages are not differently affected by the efficiency of labor, although he has elsewhere pointed out that they are. Assuming also, contrary to his own definition of circulating capital, that it is all at once distributed among laborers, he seems to suppose that the amount so distributed will depend, not upon the supposed value of what will be produced, but upon the amount of past accumulation.

He then goes on to say, "But if they aimed at obtaining actually higher wages than the rate fixed by demand and supply—the rate which distributes the whole circulating capital of the country among the entire working population—this could only be accomplished by keeping a part of their number out of employment." But there is no rate at all determined by "the whole circulating capital" as one of its factors. And there is, further, no rate, either of proportional, real, or money wages dependent directly upon the demand for labor, because the cause of any change in demand for labor is itself a corresponding change in the ratio of the demand and supply of the commodities for which labor is exchanged. Curtailment in the amount of employment does, indeed, follow any rise of proportional wages, but it is not on account of the insufficiency of circulating capital, physically available for wages, but because such rise can only be at the expense of profits, the hope of which is the sole inducement to employ labor.

There is, however, one trivial exception to the remarks I have made, which it will be well to note, although neither theoretically nor practically of much importance.

In Book V, chapter x, section 5, of Mill's work, I find the passage:

"Combinations to keep up wages are sometimes successful, in trades where the work-people are few in number, and collected in a small number of local centers. It is questionable if combinations ever had the smallest effect on the permanent remuneration of spinners or weavers; but the journeymen type-founders, by a close combination, are able, it is said, to keep up a rate of wages much beyond that which is usual in employments of equal hardness and skill; and even the tailors, a much more numerous class, are understood to have had, to some extent, a similar success. A rise of wages, thus confined to particular employments, is not (like a rise of general wages) defrayed from profits, but raises the value and price of the particular article, and falls on the consumer."

It is evident that when, in any particular trade, the rate of money-wages is raised by trades-unions, there is no rise of proportional wages; for the price of the commodity produced will soon, if not immediately, also rise enough to cover the increase in the cost of production; but there will result a rise of real wages to the laborers engaged in the supposed trade, which will be gained by them at the expense of the consumers of the article produced. In so far as such article is consumed by the poor, there is no rise in the average real wages of the class; but, in so far as it is consumed by the rich, there is such a rise, and at the expense, not of profits, but of the rich consumer. But whether this apparent rise will result in a real gain to the laboring class will depend entirely on the effect of the increased cost of such luxury upon accumulations. If the same money value is consumed as before, as it then takes fewer laborers to produce such value, some will be thrown out of employment, and the gross sum distributed as wages will be unaffected. If less is consumed and accumulations are thereby increased, there will be an absolute loss to the wages-fund; but, if unproductive consumption turns out to be increased, the laborer will gain a permanent advance in his real wages. To some small extent the latter is the ordinary result, and trades-unions have probably secured to labor some small addition to real wages in this manner; but the advantage gained, or that can be gained, is insignificant, and of very doubtful morality, consisting as it does in forcing one class to pay more than another for the same commodity—labor.

CHAPTER IX.

CO-OPERATION.

Co-operation is undoubtedly the only final solution of the labor question. Although, as I have shown, both capital and labor are equally benefited by such division of the total produce as results in such total being the largest, and that either class loses and does not gain by securing for itself any larger proportion, the actions of the individuals composing each class will not, naturally, conduce to such fair and desirable division. The conflict between individual and social interest can only cease when each individual receives profits as well as wages. We are not here concerned with the moral and industrial effects that may be expected to flow from co-operation, further than to observe that its adoption must materially increase the efficiency of labor, but that such benefit can not be looked for except as the intelligence and morality of the laboring classes are further evolved. It belongs to our subject to consider what effect its adoption will have upon the ratio of capital to population. It is evident that, when wages and profits go wholly to the same individuals, a general rise in proportional wages and corresponding decrease in profits will not, as now, at all discourage production. A general glut of material things will then be impossible, because labor will have ceased to be a commodity. Gaining in wages what he loses in profits, the inducement to the producer to go on with productive consumption will be the same. This removes the present economic check to over-accumulation. In a co-operative society excessive accumulations will be no less useless than they are in ours, but they will not be so hurtful, because they will not lead to any cessation of industry. When they occur, they will entail a loss of consumption alone, and may properly be considered as consumed unproductively, without affording any enjoyment or satisfaction; and the loss would be similar to that caused by fire or shipwreck. In such state of society accumulation would probably proceed almost, if not quite, to the annihilation of profits, but would not go beyond, as it is not in human nature to knowingly suffer a greater present deprivation for a smaller future satisfaction.

The determination of labor and capital to individual trades may then, as now, be excessive or deficient, with the result of a fall or rise of real wages and profits to the producers in them and to the corresponding benefit or loss of consumers—the producers in other trades. But this will lead only to a change and not to a cessation of employment.

At present, accumulations not only come almost exclusively from profits, but come in a disproportional degree from large profits. As a rule, the larger an individual's income, the larger the proportion of it, both relatively and absolutely, that is saved. The inequality of individual fortunes has a powerful effect in intensifying the effectiveness of the desire to accumulate. Under the present social state, the wage-receiving class are practically debarred from accumulating at all when the accumulations of the rich are excessive; the little they lay aside when the wages-fund is large is pretty certain to be unproductively consumed when the wages-fund is small, and, as we have seen, periods when it is small are the certain effect of over-accumulation by others. The effort by the rich to be richer than economic law allows, in great measure prevents the poor from ever becoming possessors of capital at all, and is the chief reason why the benefits of our progress in civilization accrue almost wholly to the fortunate few.

Under co-operation, the inequality of individual fortunes will be greatly lessened, and consequently the gross sum that can be spared and saved from incomes can not well be so great as at present, and the tendency of capital to press upon population will be correspondingly decreased. If the credit system remains after the adoption of co-operation (and it is by no means inconsistent with it), there will remain some tendency to periodicity in insolvencies, but such periods will not be accompanied by any cessation of industrial activity. There will be no loss of production, but merely a transfer from lenders to borrowers. Under complete co-operation, industrial stagnation would be impossible, but some loss of confidence might occur, as the result of disproportion in production.

It is, of course, true that the production of commodities under co-operation might be no better fitted to the needs of consumers than now, and some cessation, or rather delay, of exchanges might occur; but the consequent increase of dead stock could not then, as now, tend to any decrease in productive consumption, because then, labor being eliminated as a commodity, the demand and supply of commodities would be strictly the sum of material commodities themselves. The effect would be that any undue decrease in past unproductive consumption would soon be adjusted by a corresponding increase in future unproductive consumption, without productive consumption being either increased or decreased.

This result of co-operation, in doing away with periodic declines in industrial activity, has not, that I am aware of, been before perceived, nor could it be, until the economic effects of over-accumulation were recognized; but it affords a very powerful argument for its adoption at the earliest practicable moment. The full result will only be obtained when the change to co-operation is complete, but the severity of each crisis will be mitigated with every partial adoption of the system.

While the ultimate effect of co-operation will be to do away with the vicissitudes of business, such vicissitudes, while they remain, operate against co-operation in its competition with the present system. The proportional wages and profits combined of the individual co-operative laborer are the same in good and in bad times, and his remuneration only varies as the proportion of the commodities he produces is greater or less than the amount of the commodities the community offers in exchange for them; but the amount of employment in his trade varies with that in those trades where the product is divided, in so far at least as such products are exchanged for each other. The little accumulations, therefore, of co-operative laborers are apt to be swept away during periods of stagnation, and the co-operative enterprise destroyed through no fault of the operatives themselves, but as the result of economic causes resulting from the faults of the competing system. This, together with the present moral and intellectual status of the laboring classes, renders the establishment of any co-operative enterprise very difficult, and it is, perhaps, too soon as yet to hope for any immediate success, save in exceptional circumstances; nevertheless, the system should be kept in view, as the great and ultimate goal of political endeavor, and as the only panacea for many of our social and economic evils.

CHAPTER X.

FREE TRADE AND PROTECTION.

THE argument in favor of free trade is an exceedingly simple one—so simple, that we can not wonder at the contempt felt for the intellectual capacity of those writers who fail to comprehend it. To state it, I can not do better than to use the words of Mill, in Book III, chapter xvii, section 3, in which he says:

"We perceive in what consists the benefit of international exchange, or, in other words, foreign commerce. Setting aside its enabling countries to obtain commodities which they could not themselves produce at all, its advantage consists in a more efficient employment of the productive forces of the world. If two countries which trade together attempted, as far as was physically possible, to produce for themselves what they now import from one another, the labor and capital of the two countries would not be so productive, the two together would not obtain from their industry so great a quantity of commodities as when each employs itself in producing, both for itself and for the other, the things in which its labor is relatively most efficient. The addition thus made to the produce of the two combined constitutes the advantage of the trade."

To every word of which I cordially subscribe, except the implication that the "efficiency of labor and capital" is an equivalent term to the "efficiency of labor" alone. Any and every restriction upon commerce is undoubtedly detrimental to the productive efficiency of the labor of the world. But, when the question is discussed of the distribution of the capitalized wealth of the world and of its annual produce, I take decided issue with the English school of political economy, and I shall be able to prove that the free interchange of an agricultural with a manufacturing country not only may be, but to a large extent actually is, detrimental to the former, and that the latter may not only gain all the benefit of the increased productive efficiency, but something besides, which something is an absolute loss to the agricultural country, against which it can only protect itself by discriminating duties.

I must first ask from the reader a consideration of the inherent differences between the nature of the two great classes of industry. These differences are:

1. That agriculture can utilize much less capital than manufactures in employing a given population.

2. That the efficiency of labor is everywhere the same, or nearly so in manufacturing, but very variable in agriculture in different States, on account of the latter efficiency depending on the national margin of cultivation.

3. That the efficiency of labor is uniform in manufactures, but variable in agriculture as affected by the vicissitudes of the seasons.

1. That agriculture can utilize much less capital than manufactures in employing a given population.

The intelligent reader can hardly have failed to anticipate me in the application here of the principle of the constant tendency of capital to outstrip population. It follows, from this principle, that a country will always possess, very shortly after the need is felt, all the capital it can employ at a satisfactory rate of profit. The opening up of any new avenue for investment inevitably results in an increase of capitalized wealth; and I have further shown that such increase of capital, while it is taking place, is always accompanied by an increase of production to several times its own extent, and which continues until the new normal ratio of capital to population is attained. This result is the necessary consequence of the fall in proportional wages and rise in profits that any and every opportunity for profitable investment affords. The nature of a nation's industries, therefore, as utilizing more or less capital in proportion to population, is a vital one to its productive efficiency. This element of national productiveness has no effect upon its exchange of produce with its neighbors. Such exchange is wholly governed by the *money-cost* at which it and they can produce; and into such cost both money-wages and profits enter; but it follows, as a result of our whole argument, that, as a question of *national* profit and loss, the comparison should be simply between the money-cost of the labor that can produce the commodity at home as compared with the money-cost of that which produces the articles exchanged for the imported commodity.

To illustrate, let us suppose that in America a day's labor on the poorest land will produce wheat of the value of $1.65, $1.50 of which is paid as wages, and fifteen cents as the profit of circulating capital, at ten per cent, and that the product of one's day's labor in manufacturing woolen cloth will sell for $3.15, composed of $1.50 for wages, fifteen cents for profit on circulating capital, and $1.50 for profit on fixed capital. (For the sake of simplicity, I here suppose no fixed capital to be employed in agriculture, or, what will amount to the same thing, the profit, rent, etc., on the plant in woolen manufacture to exceed the profit of the agricultural plant by an amount equal to the wages expended in either case. The supposition is, of course, an extravagant one, and only made for the sake of enforcing the principle.) Let us likewise suppose that in England one day's labor on the poorest land will produce two thirds of what it will in America. Wages will then be one dollar per day, and the value of the produce will be $1.10. The money-price of wheat would be the same in each country—as it must always be—cost of carriage, etc., apart. Cloth, however, can be made in England, under otherwise similar conditions, for $2.10 for the product of a day's labor, one dollar of which will be wages, ten cents profit on circulating capital, and one dollar profit on fixed capital. (This is not exactly the proportion in which English fixed capital would enter into the price, but it is sufficiently exact for the purposes of this discussion. It is exact, as far as English labor and profits compose the cost of buildings, tools, etc., but not as far as raw agricultural products or imported articles enter into such cost; in fact, the amount of English fixed capital would be larger than I have stated; and such increase, whatever it would be, would entail a further loss upon America in excess of that shown by the calculation.) America can not import such cloth for less than $2.10, and may be forced to pay any price between $2.10 and $3.15.

In Book V, chapter x, section 1, Mill says:

"The amount of national loss thus occasioned (by protection) is measured by the excess of the price at which the commodity is produced over that at which it could be imported."

According to him, therefore, England gains nothing; for, as we shall see hereafter, cost of carriage, profits of importers, etc., apart, prices of agricultural produce must be the same in all countries carrying on commerce with each other. Her gain consists entirely in the rise in her margin of cultivation, caused by her importation of food, while America's gain on importing the cloth is $1.05, less the loss occasioned by any lowering of her margin of cultivation. Strictly speaking, the calculation according to Mill should take no account of the margin of cultivation, as he omitted to notice its effect upon the distribution of the gain in productiveness; as this, however, is probably only an error of omission on his part, I give him the benefit of it in my argument.

Now, this apparent gain of America is very much greater than the benefit to the world by an English laborer being employed in making cloth instead of raising wheat, and an American laborer in raising wheat instead of making cloth. As it takes the same amount of labor in either country to make the cloth, the gain in the amount of material products is solely in the increased efficiency of the labor employed in growing wheat. By the conditions of our problem this gain is fifty cents on a day's labor, and, if we accept Mill's method of calculating, America, under free trade, gains the whole money advantage of such trade and fifty-five cents besides, while England also gains a substantial advantage in her margin of cultivation only partially compensated by a smaller loss in her margin to America. This result is too absurd to be for a moment entertained. It is simply the claim that the parts can be greater than the whole. The fifty cents gain is divided into a money gain of $1.05, and that resulting from the disturbance of the two national margins of cultivation (this last is also a gain because the rise in the English margin, as a matter of fact, is greater than the fall in the American, on account of the great amount of our unoccupied fertile lands); nor can the dilemma be escaped by the claim that the extra fifty-five cents of America's gain is due to the money-cost of English capital being less than American. That is the true explanation of the fact, but, as long as there is no gain in the labor-cost of such capital, its money-cost is here a matter of indifference. The $1.05, if Mill is right, should represent a material benefit, and not a mere difference in money values; but we have seen that fifty cents, and the gain through the English margin being raised more than the American has been depressed, is the extent of the material benefit to the world, and this has now become a gain of $1.05, and the gain in the margins besides, and free-traders have the further anomaly to explain, how it happens that agricultural nations, to whom, according to them, more than the whole gain of commerce accrues, remain poor, notwithstanding the greater fertility of their soil; while manufacturing nations, who receive none of it, are the richest nations of the earth, despite their comparative sterility.

Now, let us consider the problem in consonance with the views advanced in this treatise. If America protected her woolen manufacture, as soon as she had accumulated the requisite capital, she would obtain a day's product of cloth with the same labor the product of which she formerly sold to England for $1.65; but for a day's product of English labor she was forced to pay $2.10 or over. She, therefore, formerly obtained for herself none of the benefit of the increased productiveness of labor, and lost forty-five cents besides, even when she obtained her cloth at the least possible price. England, on the other hand, sold to America the product of a day's labor for $2.10, which would have only brought her if employed in agriculture a value of $1.10. She formerly, therefore, gained the whole profit in the international exchange, and fifty cents besides, forty-five cents of which was at the expense of America, and five cents represented the profit saved on the extra circulating capital necessary to employ an American over an English laborer, or, in other words, it is the profit on the additional production of fifty cents. The American consumer does indeed pay $3.15 for an article he could import for $2.10, but the gross sum of the national profits is larger by $1.50, and the gross revenue of the whole people greater by at least forty-five cents, to which must be added the gain accruing from the consequent rise in the margin of cultivation.

Let us now change the supposition, and suppose that the cost of woolen cloth is composed of profits only to the extent of one quarter the sum paid the artisans as wages. The cost of a day's product of cloth in England will then be $1.35 and its cost at home $2.02½, the rate of profit, as before, being ten per cent alike in both countries. America will now gain thirty cents by the interchange of commodities, and England twenty cents plus the five cent profit on extra circulating capital, as before.

It would seem at first sight that America, in this case, gained the greater part of the mutual advantage, but that is not actually the case; to really do so, she should gain nearly the whole, or at least such part of the fifty cents as represents half the real advantage to the world of her employing her laborers in agriculture instead of manufactures. Proper allowance must be made for the effect of free trade upon the margin of cultivation. If England with her present population was forced to raise all her own food, her margin would be so low that she would perhaps produce, with the same amount of labor on her poorest lands, only half the produce we now get from our poorest lands. This would add twenty-five cents to her gain, in the case we have supposed, and make the total fifty cents, while a subtraction must be made from America's apparent gain of thirty cents, to allow for any lowering of her margin, on account of employing more of her labor in agriculture. If we suppose that, under protection, on the poorest lands then cultivated, ten per cent less labor than formerly was required for the same produce, her real gain under free trade would be only fifteen cents, while England's would be fifty cents; the gain to the world would then be sixty cents, composed of fifty cents former difference in the efficiency of labor, plus twenty-five cents the gain of England on the rise of her margin, and less fifteen cents the loss of America on the decline of her margin. (The five cents as before represents the profit on the increased production, and affects the distribution only, not the creation of wealth.) The rate of profit in both being the same, and all other things being equal, a manufacturing country will always gain the larger proportion of the benefit accruing from trade, and, if the article be one into the cost of which profits enter largely, it may appropriate to itself more than the whole gain, the excess being at the expense of the agricultural. If the normal rate of profit, as is usually the case, is less in the manufacturing than in the agricultural, or if the rate in both should be less than the rate we have supposed, the actual loss to the latter will be lessened, or, as the case may be, her share of the gain to the world will be increased, *but it can never quite equal one half of such gain.* I must not be understood as claiming that the element of profit, as affecting cost of production, is usually great enough of itself alone to justify protective duties, but only that it lessens very materially the proportion of the benefits of free trade to an agricultural nation as compared with what would accrue on an equal division of such benefit, and that, in connection with the effect upon the margin of cultivation, the employment of otherwise idle labor, the transmutation of common into skilled labor, and of effects upon the equation of international demand, to be hereafter noticed, it will justify protective duties in most of the instances in which they have been imposed, if the increase of mere *national* prosperity be accepted as such justification.

Whether the importation of any article, the equation of international demand being even, is actually causing a gain or loss to the country, can be ascertained pretty accurately by comparing the imported cost of such article with the *labor-cost* of producing it at home, together with an addition for the profit of circulating capital employed. From the result obtained allowance must be made for the effect of protecting or importing the article upon the margin of cultivation and upon the employment of female or other wasted labor, and the substitution of highly paid skilled for the lowly paid common labor.

There is no disputing the fact that manufacturing are uniformly richer in capitalized wealth than agricultural countries, and that, despite their lower margin of cultivation, their annual produce is nearly, if not quite, as large *per capita*. That of England and America is, as nearly as can be calculated from statistics, about the same, notwithstanding that England's margin is lower than ours by over one third. These results must be attributed wholly to moral causes, if Mill's views as to accumulation and the distribution of wealth under free trade are accepted; whereas, under the views here presented, they are the natural outcome of economic law, and afford a substantial verification of the views themselves. While to assert that England is richer than we in capitalized wealth, and produces annually an equal value *per capita*, notwithstanding our superior natural resources, because of the moral superiority and greater thriftiness of her population, will hardly avail to convince many of the soundness of Mill's deductions.

It may, however, be useful in this connection to again quote from the "Principles of Political Economy." In Book V, chapter x, section 1, I find the passage:

> "It was shown, however, in our analysis of the effects of international trade, as it had been often shown by former writers, that the importation of foreign commodities, in the common course of traffic, never takes place, except when it is, economically speaking, a *national good*, by causing the same amount of commodities to be obtained at a *smaller cost of labor and capital to the country*. To prohibit, therefore, this importation, or to impose duties which prevent it, is to render the labor and capital of the country less efficient in production than they would otherwise be, and compel a waste of the difference between the labor and capital necessary for the home production of the commodity and that which is required for producing the things with which it can be purchased from abroad."

My position is, that while the actual interchange of goods under free trade will be in accordance, as is here claimed, with the efficiency of both labor and capital, and that the interest of the world at large will also be subserved by any increase of the efficiency of its labor, the distribution of the advantage depends on other principles, and the individual interests of the different nations are regulated by other considerations, and that while a nation loses, as Mill claims, from diverting its labor to industries in which it is less efficient, it does not lose by the accompanying diversion of its capital, as such diversion, if toward industries employing greater capital than its old ones, allows otherwise impossible accumulations to be made without depressing, and even for a time increasing, the rate of profit, and the aggregate amount of profits it thus enjoys may be greatly enhanced, and that, while a part of such increase of profits will be at the expense of the home consumer, it will not all be so, but will result in a substantial increase in the net revenue of the country, sometimes less and sometimes greater, but in all cases to be offset against the loss in the efficiency of its labor, which we allow will occur, before it can be affirmed that a net loss results to such country.

And the reason that Mill failed to appreciate this result of protection can be gathered from the following passage from Book I, chapter v, section 1:

> "Had legislators been aware that *industry is limited by capital*, they would have seen that the aggregate capital of the country not having been increased, any portion of it which they by their laws had caused to be embarked in the newly-acquired branch of industry must have been withdrawn or withheld from some other; in which it gave, or would have given, employment to probably about (?) the same quantity of labor which it employs in its new occupation."

Industry is not limited by the extent of capital as defined by himself, but only by the extent of the wages-fund or capital in Ricardo's sense. On the contrary, the increase of capital, needed for protected industries, is not drawn from the wages-fund, but from dead stock, and tends to an increase of the wages-fund, because it increases the rate of profit upon which the amount of capital in the sense of this quotation—i. e., the wages-fund—really depends. The increase is ultimately drawn from the products of an increased employment of labor, to which the demand for the increase itself inevitably leads.

2. *That the efficiency of labor is everywhere the same, or nearly so, in manufacturing, but very variable in different States, in agriculture; on account of the latter efficiency depending on the national margin of cultivation.*

When I say that the efficiency of labor is everywhere the same, or nearly so, in manufacturing, I do not mean to be understood as denying or belittling the differences in the mental and physical efficiency of different races and nations of men, but I do mean to say that their comparative natural efficiency in manufacturing and in cultivating lands of the same fertility does not much differ. The labor of the rice-fed Chinamen is far less effective than that of the Anglo-Saxon, but the degree in which it is so in manufacturing is not much different from what it is in the cultivation of the soil, except, indeed, as such degree of efficiency depends upon specially acquired skill resulting from the nature of past activities, and which practice in the unaccustomed industries would soon rectify.

As Mill says in Book I, chapter vii, section 4:

"The third element which determines the productiveness of the labor of a community is the skill and knowledge therein existing; whether it be the skill and knowledge of the laborers themselves, or of those who direct their labor. No illustration is requisite to show how the efficacy of industry is promoted by the manual dexterity of those who perform mere routine processes; by the intelligence of those engaged in operations in which the mind has a considerable part; and by the amount of knowledge of natural powers and of the properties of objects, which is turned to the purposes of industry. That the productiveness of the labor of a people is limited by their knowledge of the arts of life, is self-evident; and that any progress in those arts, any improved application of the objects or powers of nature to industrial uses, enables the same quantity and intensity of labor to raise a greater produce."

But as Mill acknowledges that protective duties are defensible for the purpose of acquiring such skill and aptitude, I will not dwell upon the point, although he has been denounced for this opinion by the more ultra of his followers, further than to call attention to the fact that the temporary increase of industrial activity, that ensues upon the protection of manufactures, itself provides a fund more than sufficient for such educational purposes; and to quote the passage from Book V, chapter x, section 1, in which he thus expresses himself:

"The only case in which, on mere principles of political economy, protecting duties can be defensible, is when they are imposed temporarily (especially in a young and rising nation) in hopes of naturalizing a foreign industry, in itself perfectly suitable to the circumstances of the country. The superiority of one country over another in a branch of production often arises only from having begun it sooner. There may be no inherent advantage on one part, or disadvantage on the other, but only a present superiority of acquired skill and experience. A country which has this skill and experience yet to acquire, may in other respects be better adapted to the production than those which were earlier in the field; and, besides, it is a just remark of Mr. Rae that nothing has a greater tendency to promote improvements in any branch of production than its trial under a new set of conditions. But it can not be expected that individuals should, at their own risk, or rather to their certain loss, introduce a new manufacture, and bear the burden of carrying it on until the producers have been educated up to the level of those with whom the processes are traditional. A protecting duty, continued for a reasonable time, will sometimes be the least inconvenient mode in which the nation can tax itself for the support of such an experiment. But the protection should be confined to cases in which there is good ground of assurance that the industry which it fosters will after a time be able to dispense with it; nor should the domestic producers ever be allowed to expect that it will be continued to them beyond the time necessary for a fair trial of what they are capable of accomplishing."

Nor do I overlook the fact that some increase of the efficiency of labor engaged in manufactures follows upon their concentration in particular localities. As Mill says in Book IV, chapter ii, section 2:

"The larger the scale on which manufacturing operations are carried on, the more cheaply they can in general be performed. Mr. Senior has gone the length of enunciating, as an inherent law of manufacturing industry, that in it increased production takes place at a smaller cost, while in agricultural industry, increased production takes place at a greater cost. I can not think, however, that even in manufactures, increased cheapness follows increased production by anything amounting to a law. It is a probable and usual, but not a necessary consequence."

With this passage I fully agree, and what effect the principle has must be regarded as a deduction from the results here obtained, and neglected, not because it is unreal, but because it is of no great consequence, and perhaps nearly, if not quite, offset by other economic advantages, not elsewhere noticed by me, that ensue from the dispersion of such industries; as, for instance, the greater chance of inventions and improvements being made when the same industry is carried on by many nations and races, than when it is monopolized by one or two only.

Nor do I at all deny that climate, soil, and the mineral products of a country do, to some extent, affect the efficiency of her artisan labor. The climate of Southern Europe affords the people there advantages in the production of wine, which, from the amount of capital it engages, may be economically considered rather as a commodity than as a raw product, and the dampness of her atmosphere yields a certain advantage to England in spinning cotton, and her mines of iron and coal give her a natural advantage over her Continental neighbors in the efficiency of her artisan labor. The labor-cost is less to her than to them, but she does not possess this advantage over us, as what makes cheap iron and coal, for the purposes of this discussion, is not so much the fact that they are extracted by cheap, as by little labor. In the *natural* fertility of her mines and their abundance, she is inferior rather than superior to America. Being an industry in which the employment of capital is large, the labor-cost is much more to be considered than the money-price.

I grant at once that no endeavor should be made to overcome by means of protective duties any real natural advantages in manufacturing, possessed by foreign nations, and that, unless such advantages are inconsiderable, the attempt to overcome them will probably result in a national loss.

I am justified, however, in asserting that what differences there are in manufacturing efficiency are mainly artificial, and that the process of acquiring them may be regarded as educational; often, indeed, expensive, but justified by the result, if followed ultimately by any increment in the amount of the national produce.

As to the efficiency of labor in agriculture, the case is very different. Equal physical power and intelligence, vicissitudes of the seasons apart, will command an equal produce only from lands of the same inherent fertility. Every variation in the quality of the soil entails a variance in the crops gathered from it. When the efficiency of a nation's agricultural labor is lowered by poorer lands being put under cultivation, the efficiency of her labor employed upon the lands previously cultivated is not disturbed, but a different distribution of their produce results. Neither profits nor proportional wages are caused thereby to vary, but rent is increased at the expense of real wages, and the money value of agricultural produce continuing the same, as it may, unless affected by other causes, money-wages will also decline to the same extent as real.

Premising this much, I submit to the consideration of the reader the following extract from Mill's "Principles," Book III, chapter xxv, sections 2 and 4:

"SECTION 2. According to the preceding doctrine, a country can not be undersold in any commodity, unless the rival country has a stronger inducement than itself for devoting its labor and capital to the production of the commodity; arising from the fact that by doing so it occasions a greater saving of labor and capital, to be shared between itself and its customers—a greater increase of the aggregate produce of the world. The underselling, therefore, though a loss to the undersold country, is an advantage to the world at large; the substituted commerce being one which economizes more of the labor and capital of mankind, and adds more to their collective wealth, than the commerce superseded by it. The advantage, of course, consists in being able to produce the commodity of better quality, or with less labor (compared with other things); or perhaps, not with less labor, but in less time; with a less prolonged detention of the capital employed. This may arise from greater natural advantages (such as soil, climate, richness of mines); superior capability, either natural or acquired, in the laborers; better division of labor, and better tools or machinery. But there is no place left in this theory for the case of lower wages. This, however, in the theories commonly current, is a favorite cause of underselling. We continually hear of the disadvantage under which the British producer labors, both in foreign markets, and even in his own, through the low wages paid by his foreign rivals. These lower wages, we are told, enable, or are always on the point of enabling, them to sell at lower prices, and to dislodge the English manufacturer from all markets in which he is not artificially protected.

"Before examining this opinion on grounds of principle, it is worth while to bestow a moment's consideration upon it as a question of fact. Is it true that the wages of manufacturing labor are lower in foreign countries than in England, in any sense in which low wages are an advantage to the capitalist? The artisan of Ghent or Lyons may earn less wages in a day, but does he not do less work? Degrees of efficiency considered, does his labor cost less to his employer? Though wages may be lower on the Continent, is not the cost of labor, which is the real element in the competition, very nearly the same? That it is so, seems the opinion of competent judges, and is confirmed by the very little difference in the rate of profit between England and the Continental countries. But if so, the opinion is absurd that English producers can be undersold by their Continental rivals from this cause. It is only in America that the supposition is *prima facie* admissible. In America wages are much higher than in England, if we mean by wages the daily earnings of a laborer; but the productive power of American labor is so great—its efficiency, combined with the favorable circumstances in which it is exerted, makes it worth so much to the purchaser—that the cost of labor is lower in America than in England; as is indicated by the fact that the general rate of profits and of interest is higher.

"But is it true that low wages, even in the sense of low cost of labor, enable a country to sell cheaper in the foreign market? I mean, of course, low wages which are common to the whole productive industry of the country.

"If wages, in any of the departments of industry which supply exports, are kept artificially, or by some accidental cause, below the general rate of wages in the country, this is a real advantage in the foreign market. It lessens the comparative cost of production of those articles, in relation to others; and has the same effect as if their production required so much less labor.

"Sec. 4. These two cases of slave-labor and of domestic manufactures exemplify the conditions under which low wages enable a country to sell its commodities cheaper in foreign markets, and consequently to undersell its rivals, or to avoid being undersold by them. But no such advantage is conferred by low wages when common to all branches of industry. General low wages never caused any country to undersell its rivals, nor did general high wages ever hinder it from doing so.

"To demonstrate this, we must return to an elementary principle which was discussed in a former chapter.* General low wages do not cause low prices, nor high wages high prices, within the country itself. General prices are not raised by a rise of wages, any more than they would be raised by an increase of the quantity of labor required in all production. Expenses which affect all commodities equally, have no influence on prices. If the maker of broadcloth or cutlery, and nobody else, had to pay higher wages, the price of his commodity would rise, just as it would if he had to employ more labor; because otherwise he would gain less profit than other producers, and nobody would engage in the employment. But if everybody has to pay higher wages, or everybody to employ more labor, the loss must be submitted to; as it affects everybody alike, no one can hope to get rid of it by a change of employment; each, therefore, resigns himself to a diminution of profits, and prices remain as they were. In like manner, general low wages, or a general increase in the productiveness of labor, does not make prices low, but profits high. *If wages fall (meaning here by wages the cost of labor), why, on that account, should the producer lower his price? He will be forced, it may be said, by the competition of other capitalists who will crowd into his employment. But other capitalists are also paying lower wages, and by entering into competition with him they would gain nothing but what they are gaining already.* The rate, then, at which labor is paid, as well as the quantity of it which is employed, affects neither the value nor the price of the commodity produced, except in so far as it is peculiar to that commodity, and not common to commodities generally.

"Since low wages are not a cause of low prices in the country itself, so neither do they cause it to offer its commodities in foreign markets at a lower price. It is quite true that, if the cost of labor is lower in America than in England, America could sell her cottons

* *Supra*, Book III, chapter iv.

to Cuba at a lower price than England, and still gain as high a profit as the English manufacturer. But it is not with the profit of the English manufacturer that the American cotton-spinner will make his comparison; it is with the profits of other American capitalists. These enjoy, in common with himself, the benefit of a low cost of labor, and have accordingly a high rate of profit. This high profit the cotton-spinner must also have; he will not content himself with the English profit. It is true he may go on for a time at that lower rate, rather than change his employment; and a trade may be carried on, sometimes for a long period, at a much lower profit than that for which it would have been originally engaged in. Countries which have a low cost of labor and high profits, do not for that reason undersell others, but they do oppose a more obstinate resistance to being undersold, because the producers can often submit to a diminution of profit without being unable to live, and even to thrive, by their business. But this is all which their advantage does for them; and in this resistance they will not long persevere, when a change of times, which may give them equal profits with the rest of their countrymen, has become manifestly hopeless."

It is difficult to gather from this passage the sense in which Mill uses the term "wages"; if he means proportional wages, what he says in section 2 is true, provided general prices are not affected. If prices are lowered, the supposed country is enabled to undersell others in foreign markets; if prices are raised, they are enabled to undersell it. But in the ordinary course of affairs a change in general prices affects the rate of proportional wages more than any change in money-wages. A rise of prices, money-wages remaining the same, lowers the rate, and a fall raises it, and to such extent that in times of activity the rate is lowered notwithstanding the rise in money-wages that then occurs, and in stagnant times the rate is raised notwithstanding money-wages being cut down. A rise or fall of proportional wages is not a cause of, but is always accompanied by, because it is usually in part caused by, a fall or rise in general prices, and this latter does affect the ability to sell or be undersold in foreign markets. Mill is here speaking, probably, not of its fluctuations, but of the permanent rise of the rate which naturally occurs in nations with large accumulations. Such rise in proportional wages has, of course, no effect. But Mill persistently confounds real and proportional wages, and a fall in real wages does profoundly affect the ability of a nation to compete in foreign markets. It increases the efficiency of labor and capital in manufactures as compared with that in agriculture. When it occurs in a manufacturing nation it enables her to cheapen the manufactured goods which constitute her exports, while it lessens to an agricultural people their comparative disadvantage in manufacturing. This results from the fact that profits constitute a greater proportion of the cost of goods than of raw products. It is true, as Mill says, that "general low wages do not cause" (average) "low prices nor high wages" (average) "high prices within the country itself," but they do affect the relative prices of the commodities or products that form the bulk of a nation's exports, and do therefore affect its ability to undersell or its liability to be undersold. It is, indeed, absurd, as Mill says, to assert that a high rate of proportional wages in a manufacturing country, like England, enables her competitors to undersell her in the markets of the world; but it is absurd not for the reason Mill gives, that her ability to compete in such markets is not at all affected by the increase of the rate, but because the direct contrary of the assertion is true, and any increase in her rate of proportional wages aids her to undersell them in the articles of which her exports are mainly composed, because any lowering of the rate of profit lowers manufactured goods as compared with raw products. Mill says:

> "If wages fall (*meaning by wages the cost of labor*), why, on that account, should the producer lower his price? He will be forced, it may be said, by the competition of other capitalists who will crowd into his employment; but other capitalists are also paying lower wages, and by entering into competition with him they would gain nothing but what they are gaining already."

This latter assertion is untrue, and is equivalent to the denial that a high rate of profit will lead to any increase in industrial activity. All other capitalists are not "also paying lower wages," because many of them are not paying any wages at all, or at least are employing less labor than they might if they choose to convert more of their dead into active stock. This class would most certainly "crowd into his," and every other, "employment" on the occurrence of any fall in proportional wages, until prices are again lowered by the consequent increase of the ratio of capital to population.

But what does Mill intend by "cost of labor"? In the use of the word by his opponents, the idea is intended as applying to money, or real, not proportional wages. When it is said that labor is cheap, the meaning is, that labor of a given effectiveness can be bought for a small amount of money or other commodities. That this affects the ability of a nation to sell certain classes of goods to its neighbors is the only idea intended, and no one surely will deny that it does so. Real wages and the margin of cultivation mutually depend on each other. That real wages are small is because the margin is low, and that the margin is low is because the laborer is content to increase the population notwithstanding real wages being low.

A lowering of the margin of cultivation has no effect upon the increase of agricultural prices. That price (cost of carriage, etc., apart) must be the same the world over. When a nation, from any cause, lowers its margin, corn will bring no higher price, because, if it did, it would be soon undersold by foreign corn, and would remain in the granaries of the farmer; but the farmer can no longer sell it at the old price and pay the same money or real wages. These will, therefore, very soon be lowered, but this will also entail a corresponding lowering of the wages of artisans, and, as profits are not affected, of the prices of manufactured goods. This will affect the ability of the nation to undersell its *manufacturing* rivals. All that those who complain of "the competition of pauper labor" should mean is, that the lowness of their real wages prevents us from competing with foreigners in manufacturing. They have sometimes complained in terms that seemed to imply that such competition tended to lower the real wages of our own operatives, and, so far as they have done so, Mill is right in dismissing their complaint, and also right in asserting that (except as the equation of international demand is affected) the general ability to sell in foreign markets is not affected by the proportion between wages and profits. When, however, he draws the implication from his argument that the ability to sell particular classes of commodities is not affected, he is as certainly wrong, and, however he has understood his opponents, and however loosely they have expressed themselves, this is all that is really necessary to the argument in favor of protection, showing as it does that if there is any inherent benefit to a nation, other things being equal, in diverting its industry from agriculture to manufactures, such advantage can not be realized if an unrestricted international interchange is allowed.

I have already proved that such an advantage exists, but it may not be useless to again do so by another illustration:

Let us suppose, then, two peoples of equal population, say of one million laborers, with an equal rate of profit, say ten per cent; the margin of cultivation in one being so much lower than in the other that, by an equal amount of physical effort on the poorest lands of each, only half the produce of the other was obtained by the more sterile nation. Let us further suppose that the amount of gold in each was such that a bushel of wheat brought the same price in both (which result would be a necessary consequence of their trading with each other a short time, whatever the original distribution of gold). Now, let us suppose these nations to be completely isolated from each other and from all the world, and the problem is, to ascertain how the annual product of one would compare with that of the other, and then to ascertain how interchanging commodities will affect them. If we take it for granted, as would be nearly the case, that the consumption of food would be the same in each, the more fertile would employ a larger proportion of its labor as artisans than the other. Let us suppose that two fifths of its population raise its food, the remaining three fifths will be engaged in manufactures. In the more sterile, four fifths will then be employed in farming and only one fifth as artisans, leaving rent for the moment out of the account. The richer country will produce annually two fifths more than the sterile of material commodities, less the excess of the agricultural rent of the sterile over that of the fertile country, and this excess (of two fifths less rent) will be wholly in manufactured commodities. What the excess of rent will be, can not be calculated. It might be very little, or even in favor of the more fertile country, but it could hardly be so great as to entirely absorb the difference in the productive capacity of the two nations. Let us suppose it to be one fifth, although one tenth would probably be a liberal estimate. The fertile nation would then be only twenty per cent better off than the sterile in its productive efficiency, and the latter would employ three fifths of its population in raising food and two fifths in manufacturing.

The exchangeable or gold value of their produce would, however, vary much more. Supposing profits in both at ten per cent, and that, on the average, manufactures employed an excess of plant over farming equal to twice the annual amount of manufacturing wages, the gold value of the product of three hundred working days (wages being one dollar in the sterile, and two dollars in the fertile land) would be as follows:

IN THE FERTILE COUNTRY.

Wages of 400,000 men 300 days, at $2.00, in agriculture	$240,000,000
Wages of 600,000 men 300 days, at $2.50, in manufactures	450,000,000
(I here suppose the skilled labor of artisans to be worth twenty-five per cent more than unskilled agricultural labor.)	
Profits on circulating capital	69,000,000
Profits on fixed capital	90,000,000
Profits on rentals	6,000,000
Rent (assumed)	60,000,000
	$915,000,000

For convenience in calculating, I assume the rental to be paid in advance by the farmer.

IN THE STERILE COUNTRY.

Wages of 600,000 men 300 days, at $1.00, in agriculture	$180,000,000
Wages of 400,000 men 300 days, at $1.25, in manufactures	150,000,000
Profits on circulating capital	33,000,000
Profits on fixed capital	30,000,000
Profits on rentals	12,000,000
Rent, by supposition one fifth the value of 300,000,000 days' agricultural labor in addition to the rental of the fertile country	120,000,000
	$525,000,000

This excess of $390,000,000 in the gold value of its products does not express, however, the real advantage in material things that the fertile country possesses. The gold value and the real amount of the agricultural produce is the same, agricultural profits, wages, and rent together amounting to the same sum, $330,000,000. The gold value of manufactured goods is, however, twice as great in the fertile as in the sterile country; her real advantage is, therefore, less than these figures show. The real amount is the product of 200,000 laborers employed as artisans for 300 days, together with the profits of the fixed and circulating capital. With profits and wages as supposed, the value of such product in the fertile country would be $195,000,000, or $97,500,000 in the sterile.

Now let us suppose these countries to commence trading together. At first the sterile nation would export goods and import gold; when that had affected prices sufficiently, it would commence to import food and raw products also, and to divert its labor from agriculture to manufactures, while industry in the fertile country would take the reverse direction. If population remained stationary and there were no cost of carriage to be considered, the ultimate result would be that the margin of cultivation would be the same in both countries, except such small difference as would lead the sterile country to continue importing food, which we will disregard. If we further suppose the gradation in the fertility of the lands previously cultivated to be the same in both, the sterile country would have previously cultivated twice the land that the fertile did, less the difference expressed by its greater rental, which we have assumed as half such excess. The sterile country would then attain the same margin by throwing the poorest third of her land out of cultivation, if we suppose, as would probably be the case, that, on account of the abundance of her fertile land, the increase of agricultural industry did not lower the margin in the fertile country.

The sterile land would now employ two fifths of its labor agriculturally and three fifths in manufactures, and the fertile only two fifths as artisans and three fifths as farm-hands; its artisans being then employed in the coarser manufactures, requiring but little capital, which circumstance, though greatly assisting my argument, I will leave out of the calculation.

Money, real and proportional wages, would now be the same in both countries. Prices of both raw products and goods would also be the same, except, of course, to such extent as would lead to a continuance of commercial relations, which difference I disregard in the calculation below. Let us compute the real, now also the exchangeable, value of the annual product of the two nations:

THE FERTILE COUNTRY.

Wages of 600,000 men 300 days, at $1.60, in agriculture	$288,000,000
(The money value of a day's wages will be such that the joint product of the two countries will have the same money value as before, as no increase or decrease of gold has occurred. The rates here supposed bring about this result as nearly as any that could be conveniently used.)	
Wages of 400,000 men 300 days, at $2.00, in manufactures	240,000,000
Profits on circulating capital	52,800,000
Profits on fixed capital	48,000,000
Profits on rentals	6,000,000
Rent as before	60,000,000
	$694,800,000

THE STERILE COUNTRY.

Wages of 400,000 men 300 days, at $1.60, in agriculture	$192,000,000
Wages of 600,000 men 300 days, at $2.00, in manufactures	360,000,000
Profits on circulating capital	55,200,000
Profits on fixed capital	72,000,000
Profits on rentals	6,000,000
Rent, now only	60,000,000
	$745,200,000

The total production of the sterile country is now greater than that of the fertile by a value of $50,400,000, which, divided by $2.60 (the cost in profits and wages of a day's product of artisan labor), gives the material product of 19,384,615 days of artisan labor; whereas the relative advantage formerly belonged to the fertile country to the extent of 60,000,000 days of such labor. The total relative gain of the manufacturing country is 79,384,615 days of artisan labor, but the total gain to them both by their intercourse can not be more than the gain in efficiency of the 200,000 laborers transferred from manufacturing to agriculture in the fertile country. This gain is of half their labor, and amounts to the products of 30,000,000 days' labor employed in agriculture, which is equal to 24,000,000 days of artisan labor. The manufacturing country has obtained. as the fruits of free trade, and solely at the expense of the agricultural, the products of 55,384,615 days of artisan labor, and the whole gain, besides, of the increased efficiency of the united labor of them both.

I have supposed, of course, an extreme though perfectly permissible case. As the effect of the intercourse, population would advance so as to keep the margin of cultivation considerably lower in the sterile country than in the fertile, and as far as this happened her relative and absolute gain would be lessened. The rate of profit, the comparative efficiency of labor in manufacturing, the equation of international demand, with its consequent indebtedness of the fertile to the sterile nation, would all affect the result, and none of these causes can be so approximately estimated as to give any value to computations based upon them. I will only say of them that the equation of international demand, as we shall hereafter see, will also tend to the benefit of the manufacturing nation, and that any lowering of the margin of cultivation in the agricultural land will be an added detriment to it and to the world, so that, in practice, whenever the two margins became the same, the loss of the latter country through free trade would be much greater, and the gain to the world less, than I have figured.

The results I have obtained in my calculations are inexplicable if Mill is right as to the distribution of advantage under free trade. He certainly is right, however, if his views as to capital, here combated, are correct. In Book III, chapter xviii, section 2, he says:

"It is even possible to conceive an extreme case, in which the whole of the advantage resulting from the interchange would be reaped by one party, the other country gaining nothing at all."

He is here discussing the equation of international demand, and what he says is true as affecting that question, but is certainly less than true as affecting international trade, as we have seen in the instance supposed. He everywhere assumes, and sometimes distinctly asserts, that the effect of international exchange upon the distribution of wealth can not exceed the limits of the increased product that results from the same cause.

In this variance of my view from that of Mill I find that I, rather than he, am sustained by the authority of Ricardo. The appeal to his decision can not be very definite, as the point had not then arisen in the discussion of the subject; but, in his whole chapter on foreign trade, Ricardo scrupulously, and with apparent care, discusses the subject of international exchange in terms of labor only, whereas Mill as carefully does so in terms of both labor and capital. Ricardo's exemplification of the subject contains absolutely nothing in conflict with the views here set forth, although there is much in these views not to be found in his pages. He considers the sole advantage of foreign trade to consist in the exchange of the products of a smaller for those of a larger amount of labor, without any regard to the profits of capital. Mill considers it to consist in the exchange of a smaller amount of money-wages and profits for what would otherwise cost a larger amount of money-wages and profits;

while I hold that the comparison must be made between the labor expended on the products exchanged for the imported commodity, and the labor that could have produced such commodity at home. My view, therefore, almost coincides with that of Ricardo, and the weight of his authority is decidedly against Mill.

Ricardo also distinctly acknowledged, although he did not pursue the subject to its conclusion, that the distribution between the two nations of their joint product may be to the absolute disadvantage of one of them, notwithstanding an increase of such joint product. In chapter xxv, on "Colonial Trade," p. 205, he says:

> "That the loss sustained through a disadvantageous distribution of labor in two countries may be beneficial to one of them, while the other is made to suffer more than the loss actually belonging to such a distribution, has been stated by Adam Smith himself; which, if true, will at once prove that a measure which may be greatly hurtful to a colony may be partially beneficial to the mother-country."

Here is a most positive accordance with my view, and a disagreement from that of Mill. The wonderful deductive power of Ricardo's mind preserved him from most of Mill's errors. Starting from capital as he defined it, I find little in his work to object to, except the definition of capital itself, and the fact that occasionally he has used the term in a broader signification than his definition allows. It is Mill, and not I, who differs from him, because he has applied Ricardo's deductions to a definition of capital not contemplated by him, and from which the deductions by no means follow, or were intended by Ricardo to follow.

While, therefore, the proportional cost of labor to some extent determines the nature of a nation's industries, the real or money cost does so to a much greater degree; and I am entitled to affirm that a high rate of real or money wages diverts the industry of a nation into those channels where it derives the least benefit from the use and increase of its capital, and where its labor is more wastefully, because more unskillfully, applied.

3. That the efficiency of labor is uniform in manufactures, but variable in agriculture as affected by the vicissitudes of the seasons.

This difference between agriculture and manufactures will be of importance later on, as affecting the equation of international demand, and is only noted here to preserve the symmetry of the argument.

CHAPTER XI.

THE EQUATION OF INTERNATIONAL DEMAND.

In the discussion of this question, Mill, in Book III, chapter xviii, section 4, says:

"If, therefore, it be asked what country draws to itself the greatest share of the advantage of any trade it carries on, the answer is, the country *for whose productions there is in other countries the greatest demand, and a demand the most susceptible of increase from additional cheapness.* In so far as the productions of any country possess this property, the country obtains all foreign commodities at less cost. It gets its imports cheaper, the greater the intensity of the demand in foreign countries for its exports. It also gets its imports cheaper, the less the extent and intensity of its own demand for them. The market is cheapest to those whose demand is small. A country which desires few foreign productions, and only a limited quantity of them, while its own commodities are in great request in foreign countries, will obtain its limited imports at extremely small cost—that is, in exchange for the produce of a very small quantity of its labor and capital."

With all of which I, of course, agree. When, however, in section 8, in further elucidation of the subject, he says—

"The only general law, then, which can be laid down, is this. The values at which a country exchanges its produce with foreign countries depend on two things: First, on the amount and extensibility of their demand for its commodities, compared with its demand for theirs; and, secondly, on the capital which it has to spare, from the production of domestic commodities, for its own consumption. The more the foreign demand for its commodities exceeds its demand for foreign commodities, and the less capital it can spare to produce for foreign markets, compared with what foreigners spare to produce for its markets, the more favorable to it will be the terms of interchange; that is, the more it will obtain of foreign commodities in return for a given quantity of its own.

"But these two influencing circumstances are in reality reducible to one; for the capital which a country has to spare from the production of domestic commodities for its own use is in proportion to its own demand for foreign commodities; *whatever proportion of its collective income it expends in purchases from abroad, that same proportion of its capital is left without a home market for its productions.* The new element, therefore, which, for the sake of scientific correctness, we have introduced into the theory of international values, does not seem to make any very material difference in the practical result"—

I do not wholly follow him. He must surely be wrong when he affirms, "Whatever proportion of its collective income it expends in purchases from abroad, that same proportion of its capital is left without a home market for its productions." This would only be true of a nation whose exports were equally composed of goods and raw produce, or rather of one the value of whose exports was composed of profit to the same degree as its articles for home consumption. But we have seen that the nature of a nation's industries and exports depends mainly upon its margin of cultivation. An over-populated country will export a much larger proportion of articles, the price of which is due largely to profits, than an under-populated. A mutual and equal decrease of demand between them will, therefore, liberate less labor and more capital in the manufacturing than in the agricultural country. This will lower profits and decrease production in the former, and raise profits and increase production in the latter, until the ratio of capital to population is readjusted. Conversely, a mutual and equal increase of demand will raise profits and increase production in the former, and lower profits and decrease production in the latter. A growing trade between them will result in a larger proportion of benefit to the manufacturing and smaller proportion of benefit to the agricultural nation. To illustrate, let us suppose that the value of the exports of America to England, being mainly raw produce, is composed of eighty per cent wages and twenty per cent profits, the value of her articles of home consumption being seventy per cent wages and thirty per cent profits, while the value of England's exports to America, mainly highly manufactured goods, is composed fifty per cent of wages and fifty per cent of profits, her articles of home consumption being of sixty-five per cent wages and thirty-five per cent profits. On a decrease of trade between the two nations, England would be obliged to employ sixty-five laborers to utilize the same capital that formerly employed only fifty, while America would have to employ only seventy to utilize the capital that formerly employed eighty. I think I have conclusively shown that the effect of this would be, through the competition of capital in England, to raise proportional wages there, and to lower them in America through the competition of laborers. This could not but lead to a decrease in the industrial activity of England, and an increase in that of America.

"These two influencing circumstances" are not therefore really reducible to one. A mutual and equal decrease of demand would, in some degree, affect the equation of international demand between England and America, as it would certainly tend to lower the price of English commodities and raise the price of American—a result, as far as it goes, beneficial to us, while an increase in such demand would have a contrary tendency, and be in some degree hurtful to American interests. The more extensive, therefore, the commerce that is carried on between England and America, the more will the equation of international demand incline in favor of the former, because, as Mill says:

> "The less capital it (a nation) can spare to produce for foreign markets, compared with what foreigners spare to produce for its markets, the more favorable to it will be the terms of interchange."

Later on, in Book V, chapter x, section 1, Mill acknowledges this effect, though for somewhat other reasons than those here advanced. With those reasons I agree, and quote the passage as illustrating another and admitted advantage that may result from protection, and which, although not of itself sufficient to justify that policy, augments, in no inconsiderable degree, the sum of the various advantages which are, in most instances, its complete justification:

> "Those who have not well considered the subject are apt to suppose that our exporting an equivalent in our own produce, for the foreign articles we consume, depends on contingencies—on the consent of foreign countries to make some corresponding relaxation of their own restrictions, or on the question whether those from whom we buy are induced by that circumstance to buy more from us; and that if these things, or things equivalent to them, do not happen, the payment must be made in money. Now, in the first place, there is nothing more objectionable in a money payment than in payment by any other medium, if the state of the market makes it the most advantageous remittance; and the money itself was first acquired, and would again be replenished, by the export of an equivalent value of our own products. But, in the next place, a very short interval of paying in money would so lower prices as either to stop a part of the importation, or raise up a foreign demand

for our produce sufficient to pay for the imports. I grant that this disturbance of the equation of international demand would be in some degree to our disadvantage, in the purchase of other imported articles; and that a country *which prohibits some foreign commodities does, cæteris paribus, obtain those which it does not prohibit, at a less price* than it would otherwise have to pay. To express the same thing in other words: a country which destroys or prevents altogether certain branches of foreign trade, thereby annihilating a general gain to the world, which would be shared in some proportion between itself and other countries, does, in some circumstances, draw to itself, at the expense of foreigners, a larger share than would else belong to it of the gain arising from that portion of its foreign trade which it suffers to subsist. But even this it can only be enabled to do, if foreigners do not maintain equivalent prohibitions or restrictions against its commodities."

Again, in Book III, chapter xviii, section 8, Mill goes on to say:

"It still appears that the countries which carry on their foreign trade on the most advantageous terms are those whose commodities are most in demand by foreign countries, and which have themselves the least demand for foreign commodities. From which, among other consequences, it follows that the richest countries, *cæteris paribus*, gain the least by a given amount of foreign commerce; since, having a greater demand for commodities generally, they are likely to have a greater demand for foreign commodities, and thus modify the terms of interchange to their own disadvantage. Their aggregate gains by foreign trade, doubtless, are generally greater than those of poorer countries, since they carry on a greater amount of such trade, and gain the benefit of cheapness on a larger consumption; but their gain is less on each individual article consumed."

We fail to see that this necessarily follows. The proportion of a nation's income which will be expended upon imported commodities does not so much depend upon the gross amount of such income, nor upon the average income *per capita* of her population, as upon the greater or less variety of her own products, which is always less in agricultural than in manufacturing countries. If we suppose three nations one of whom was willing and able to import a value of $100,000,000, and the other two only $80,000,000 each, it is perfectly conceivable that the rich nation might exchange $50,000,000 with each, and they $30,000,000 with each other, and the equation not be at all affected thereby. If the richer nation desired to import $110,000,000, whether she could do so, without affecting the equation, would depend entirely upon the willingness of the others to transfer their demand from each other to her. If, indeed, one nation should demand all the exportable produce that other nations could spare, the equation would be affected disastrously for her, but this could not occur simply from the greater wealth of any nation, but also from its increase of territory, in which case, owing to the increase in the variety of its own industries, the proportion of its demand for foreign products would be correspondingly lessened.

But it is not always true that the aggregate demand of rich countries (by which is here meant, countries of large capital in proportion to their population) is greater than that of poorer ones. The demand is likely to be not in proportion to the capital, but to the annual produce, of different nations. England is far richer than we, but her annual produce *per capita* is supposed to be about the same. As affecting our trade with her, little or no effect upon the equation can be attributed to the comparative wealth of the two nations.

The equation is, however, profoundly affected by the proportion in which the total income of the two countries is divided between the wages and capitalist classes. As a country engages in manufacturing chiefly because its margin of cultivation is low, its real wages and total wages-fund will be considerably less than the real wages and wages-fund of an agricultural country. Now, it will not be disputed that the larger the income of any individual, the smaller the proportion of it will be expended by him for food, and the larger for manufactured goods. The average incomes of American laborers are much larger than the average incomes of English laborers. Their demand will, therefore, be somewhat greater for manufactured goods. The English capitalists enjoy on the average a greater income and a greater gross sum of profits than the American; and, consequently, a larger proportion of their demand will be for goods and a smaller for food. In each country the relatively preponderating class will exert a proportionally larger demand for English goods than they will for American products. This can not but result in the demand for English products being greater than the demand for American,* and must incline the equations very considerably in England's favor. It can be stated, as a general law of international demand, that the demand of a country with a low margin of cultivation for the products of a country with a high margin will be less than the reciprocal demand for its goods by the other, and, *cæteris paribus*, the greater share of the benefit of their mutual intercourse will accrue to the more sterile country.

I would refer to the following passage from Mill's

* Whether the greater demand for English goods comes from America or England makes no difference, as the greater the English demand for her own goods the less she can spare of them for export. It is the total demand which will sustain the prices of English goods somewhat above what would otherwise be their natural level, and correspondingly depress the prices of American produce, and it is through these prices that the equation of international demand would be affected and expressed.

"Principles," as explaining and elucidating international demand, Book III, chapter xx, section 3:

"From the preceding considerations, it appears that those are greatly in error who contend that the value of money, in countries where it is an imported commodity, must be entirely regulated by its value in the countries which produce it, and can not be raised or lowered in any permanent manner unless some change has taken place in the cost of production at the mines. On the contrary, any circumstance which disturbs the equation of international demand with respect to a particular country, not only may, but must, affect the value of money in that country—its value at the mines remaining the same. The opening of a new branch of export trade from England; an increase in the foreign demand for English products, either by the natural course of events or by the abrogation of duties; a check to the demand in England for foreign commodities, by the laying on of import duties in England or of export duties elsewhere—these, and all other events of similar tendency, would make the imports of England (bullion and other things taken together) no longer an equivalent for the exports; and the countries which take her exports would be obliged to offer their commodities, and bullion among the rest, on cheaper terms, in order to re-establish the equation of demand; and thus England would obtain money cheaper and would acquire a generally higher range of prices. Incidents the reverse of these would produce effects the reverse—would reduce prices; or, in other words, raise the value of precious metals. It must be observed, however, that money would thus be raised in value only with respect to home commodities; in relation to all imported articles it would remain as before, since their values would be affected in the same way and in the same degree with its own. A country which, from any of the causes mentioned, gets money cheaper, obtains all its other imports cheaper likewise."

I have heretofore been discussing the question of free trade or protection under the supposition that the equation of international demand did not operate unfavorably to agricultural nations; but we now see that a further addition to the possible benefits of protection, beyond those already enumerated, is to be found in the fact that protection tends to adjust that equation more to the advantage of an agricultural country. Even if, under free trade, such country suffered no loss in the gross amount of its profits, and from its labor being diverted from highly paid and skilled to more poorly paid and unskilled industries, and from its female labor being less utilized, it could still hope for little or none of the benefit accruing from the greater efficiency of its own labor, as its just share of this benefit would be all or nearly all transferred, by the operation of the laws of international demand, to the manufacturing nations with which it traded.

I have thus far been exclusively considering the commercial intercourse that takes place between civilized nations, in which the augmentation and application of capital are affected only by economic and not by moral causes, at least to any appreciable degree. It may be well in this connection to consider the effects of free trade between two such countries as England and India. The margin of cultivation in India is much lower than in England, and yet she remains an agricultural land, and depends upon the latter very largely for her manufactured goods. Ostensible profits are very high. This is largely owing to the insecurity of capital, but, after every deduction is made on that account, the real rate of profit is undoubtedly higher than in England. Under a natural and civilized state of affairs she would manufacture for England, and not England for her, despite this last circumstance. Why does she not do so? There are no economic reasons, except her disadvantage in the cost of coal, which is very far from balancing her advantage in the low money and real cost of her labor, and that there, as in most uncivilized countries, population presses upon capital instead of capital upon population. Her seasons of industrial depression are never the result of a plethora of dead stock, but of an actual insufficiency of all her stock to support her laborers from harvest to harvest; and although I have not the statistics at hand to prove the assertion, and doubt whether such statistics exist, I venture to assert that in such periods her rate of profit, if it could be ascertained, would be found to advance instead of to recede, as it does in civilized nations, in their periods of depression. That population presses upon capital is the effect wholly of moral causes, but it renders India physically incapable of accumulating the capital required for manufacturing. If the security afforded by English rule leads gradually to an increase in the desire to accumulate, and her capital once gains a foothold in manufacturing, it will not be long before England will be forced to shut out her competition by protective duties, as, I understand, she practically does now by discouraging, by every means in her power, any diversion of Indian industry from agriculture to manufactures.

While the rate of profit in India is higher than in England, the share of the gross product that accrues to capital is less, because her fixed capital and dead stock are many times less than her circulating, while in England the fixed is several times the amount of circulating wealth. On account of the scarcity of the precious metals there, exchange between the two countries should be in favor of India, and for a long time was so, as was shown by her continued import of silver. Lately, however, the exchange has turned in England's favor, and it has done so on account of the extent of the remittances from India to England as interest on English capital there invested. Whatever benefit India derives from such investments is subject to the serious drawback of the disturbance of the exchange and equation to her injury. If, therefore, English capital should be further invested in manufacturing in India, the result would be a further disturbance of the equation that would leave to India little or none of the benefit of having factories established in her midst. Now there is a positive loss to the world in England's manufacturing for India. There would be a great gain in industrial efficiency if India should divert some of her labor from agriculture to manufactures, and England or some other country transform an equivalent number of her artisans into agriculturists. Mill must, therefore, be wrong when he asserts that the equation of international demand can only vary *within the limits of the advantage* to the world afforded by free trade, as the equation is here in favor of England, notwithstanding a *loss* to the world of productive efficiency. Any tribute paid by one country to another, whether in the shape of a tax or of the interest and profit of invested capital, affects the equation to the injury of the paying nation, independent of any other cause or limit.

The advantage which England derives from her conquest of India is not only the profit of the ensuing trade, but also the opportunity afforded her for investment there, which, by draining off English capital, has not only added to her income the interest and profits of such capital, which otherwise she could not have accumulated, but has also, by sustaining the rate of profit at home, enabled her to increase her industrial activity and the amount of her annual product. She has supplanted with her own capital the capital which India would naturally have accumulated if she had enjoyed a like security under her own rulers, and, in so far as she has done so, she has absorbed at the expense of India the benefits of the security she has conferred upon her.

As long as the equation of international demand between the two countries remains as it is, the value of the home commodities of India can not advance and may recede, and the value of her imported commodities can not recede and may advance. But the implication in what I have heretofore said, that the equation is equalized when gold or silver ceases to pass between two countries, is untrue. The flow of specie or bullion stops when any equilibrium of demand is reached, however disadvantageous such equilibrium may be to one of the countries. The equation is only really equal when there is an equal division of the benefits of the international exchange. England at present derives in her commerce with India all or nearly all of this benefit; indeed, the assertion may be hazarded that she enjoys more than all, and yet the equation has reached an equilibrium or rather yet inclines to the favor of England—whereas the bulk of the benefit would naturally go to India, until the consequent influx of specie had raised the prices of her raw produce nearly to the same level as prices of raw produce in England. If India should protect her own (not borrowed) capital, invested in factories, this state of affairs would quickly cease. Her demand on England would be lessened, and the equation readjusted in her favor, and it would not attain an equilibrium until she had received her proper share of the metallic currency of the world. In her case the benefits of a protective policy would not be liable to any offset on account of a loss in the efficiency of her labor, as it would result in a positive gain in this respect. But when, as the result of protection, her manufacturers were once firmly established, her interests would be advanced by the general adoption of free trade, as she would then be able to undersell in manufactures most of the nations of the earth, and appropriate to herself those industries that allow the utilizations of the largest capitals and the employment of her labor in the better paid avocations, and which employ female labor to the greatest degree.

There is little danger to European nations of India pursuing any such course. England will not allow her to do so, as long as she is able to control her action, and the anarchy that would follow a release from English rule would yet more effectually prevent it. But, while India is helpless, China and Japan are not. They have already entered upon an industrial competition with Europeans, and have driven them from every field upon which they have entered as competitors. China is now doing all her own sea-board carrying-trade, and has even established a steamship line to our shores. She and Japan also will soon be erecting cotton, silk, and woolen mills, and, when they do, competition with them by English and American labor will be utterly futile under free trade. They will as certainly monopolize our markets as their own. Their margin of cultivation is too low for us to contend with them in the most desirable departments of human endeavor. When they have adapted their capital and population to the new economic conditions, they will obtain for themselves not only all the benefit of the increased efficiency of labor, but much more, at our expense; until, finally, our more rapid increase of population shall have reduced our margin to theirs, and reduced the moral and physical status of our laboring population to that of their coolies. The remorseless competition of free trade will bestow more than all the advantages of international intercourse upon the lowest and least developed races of mankind.

Returning again to the consideration of the exchange between civilized nations, I would call attention to another circumstance affecting the equation between manufacturing and agricultural nations, viz., the third inherent difference I have noted in the last chapter between the efficiency of the two kinds of labor. I then said:

"*3. That the efficiency of labor is uniform in manufactures, but variable in agriculture, as affected by the vicissitudes of the seasons.*"

It is a fully conceded fact that the adjustment of the equation of demand and supply acts more violently on the prices of food and raw products than on the prices of manufactured goods. Not only are they more perishable, and not so capable of being held for a better market, but the demand neither increases nor decreases in proportion to their cheapness and dearness. That this affects the equilibrium of the equation to the advantage of manufacturing countries, Mill himself allows in the quotation I have made from him at the beginning of this chapter; * and how important this concession is, can not but strike any one familiar with his illustration of the adjustment of the equation in the supposed trade between England and Germany, in cloth and linen. In this illustration he shows how the whole benefit may accrue to the nation whose demand for the products of the other increases least as the effects of cheapness, and certainly the demand

* Book III, chapter xviii, section 4: "If, therefore, it be asked what country draws to itself the greatest share of the advantage of any trade it carries on, the answer is, the country for whose productions there is in other countries the greatest demand, and *a demand the most susceptible of increase from additional cheapness.*"

of a manufacturing nation for agricultural produce fulfills this condition.

But the efficiency of agricultural labor being so largely determined by the vicissitudes of the seasons, produces another effect in addition to this. A high price of manufactured goods immediately leads to and is accompanied by a great increase of production, and such high price is realized on a greater product; but a high price of raw products is caused and accompanied by a small amount of production, and is only realized on a relatively lesser product. This effect, to be sure, is partly compensated by the high price of raw products being longer sustained than the high price of goods, because the supply which will eventually lower the price can not so soon be obtained. It is not wholly so compensated, because the supply of goods comes gradually, and, on account of the greater employment of labor it calls for, unproductive consumption is increased, and any increase of unproductive consumption tends to longer sustain prices and profits. The increase of the supply of raw produce and food comes suddenly. It is usually affected at once, as soon as a new harvest is gathered; but, unlike a scarcity of goods, a scarcity of raw produce and food does not lead to any increase in the employment of labor, but rather to a decrease, unless, indeed, it is continued through several seasons, and then the effectual demand of laborers is greatly lessened, even though more are employed, on account of the consequent fall in their real wages. The scarcity price is not, therefore, at all sustained by an increase of unproductive consumption, and as the profits of different industries in different nations do not so strongly tend to equality as do the profits of different industries within a nation, it follows that fluctuations in value will tend, on the whole, to benefit manufacturing rather than agricultural profits and prices.

The effect upon the equation of international demand of the inherent differences between agriculture and manufactures is, as far as I am aware, a result that has hardly been noticed, much less discussed, by economists. Mill does barely touch upon the subject in discussing the cost of bullion in Book III, chapter xix, section 2, where he says:

"Countries whose exportable produce consists of the *finer manufactures*, obtain bullion, as well as all other foreign articles, *cæteris paribus*, at less expense than countries which export nothing but bulky raw produce."

But neither here nor elsewhere has he given to the subject much consideration.

I am by no means confident that I have enumerated all of the causes which affect the equation to the detriment of an agricultural people; much, doubtless, that I have failed to observe might be elucidated by further discussion; but I have shown that the equilibrium of the equation will certainly be reached at a point that will yield the largest share of benefit to manufacturing nations. What are the limits within which the equation must somewhere settle? Mill asserts that such limits are supplied by the increased efficiency of labor and capital due to international trade—Ricardo, to the increased efficiency of labor alone. The gain to the world is surely no more than the increase in the efficiency of labor. Indeed, I utterly fail to comprehend the expression, "increased efficiency of capital" as relating to the nationality of capital. It can not refer to the rate of profit; that has to do with the division of the product, not its amount. The same material amount (not value) of fixed capital (and it is fixed capital which mainly concerns us here) will employ the same amount of labor, of equal skill and efficiency, in one country as it will in another. It is indeed true that a country in which the *value* of such capital is the least can produce manufactured goods at a correspondingly smaller money cost, but that does not affect the totality of the world's products, but only their division. All variations in "the efficiency of capital" are really variations in the efficiency of labor. Mill is more accurate in his statement than Ricardo, but neither of them is right. The limits of the fluctuations of the equation of international exchange are the prices at which the articles under consideration can be produced in the exporting and in the importing country. As far as such prices depend upon economic causes, such economic causes do not include the "efficiency of capital," but are mainly the respective margins of cultivation, and in some slight degree the rate of proportional wages; but sometimes, as in the case of England and India, moral causes practically remove all limits by preventing the accumulation of the capital necessary to the most advantageous employment of labor. Mill and Ricardo themselves affirm that the limits I have claimed are the true ones, and only assert the gain in efficiency to be also the limit, because they consider the two to be identical. I have already shown the absurd conclusions to which the supposition of their identity leads.*

Now, the equation of international demand can not cause imported food and raw products (cost of carriage, etc., apart) to sell at a less price than the food and raw produce raised at home, unless such food and raw produce are of a nature utterly unfitted for the national soil

* See chapter v, on "Free Trade and Protection."

and climate, and are not raised at all by the importing nation. The importing nation, nevertheless, obtains an advantage by such importations, which it expends in raising its margin or increasing its population, but such advantage is not expressed at all by a difference of price as affected by the equation we are considering. Trade with an agricultural nation will, of course, lower the price of food and raw products, but it will do so to exactly the same extent, whether the equation be in favor of or against the nation that imports them. How the equation stands will show itself entirely in the price which such nation obtains from the agricultural nations with which she trades for the manufactures she exports, and that price will vary between that at which she could afford to sell the goods immediately after they were produced and the price at which the country to which she exports her goods could produce them at home. Now, if her margin has been raised by the trade, she can not afford to sell her goods at so low a price as before; and if her margin should be raised to nearly the same point as that of the agricultural country, she could afford to sell her goods at very little below the cost at which the agricultural country could produce them herself. As her margin approaches that of the other, the limits narrow within which the equation can find an equilibrium, and, when the margins became the same, trade would cease between the two nations, except in those articles in which one or the other of them possessed a natural advantage of soil or climate, or an acquired advantage of skill. Each nation would produce for herself both the raw produce and the manufactured goods, in the production of which she labored under no real disadvantage. Such a result could only occur as a consequent of a comparative depopulation of the manufacturing country. Although such depopulation would result in a diminution of the gross amount of its annual produce, the product *per capita* might or might not be increased. During all this process the equilibrium of the equation might remain steady, as it is supposable, for instance, that the manufacturing country might continue all the time to sell its exports at the lowest price at which it could produce them, and, though the price of such goods would constantly advance, the equilibrium of the equation would not be thereby disturbed. The equation itself would become more and more beneficial to the agricultural country, but it could never attain more than its just share of the benefit, and that at the expense of the lowering of its margin.

But how can it be determined that the prices at which goods are interchanged between nations are such that neither suffers from its demand for the other's goods being greater than the demand of the other for its goods? Such a state of affairs exists when each nation pays for its imports the price at which the other can afford to sell them to it, with the ordinary profit, immediately after, or at a corresponding and equal distance of time from, their production. If either nation pays the other a greater price than this, the equation is against it to exactly that extent.

To make this point plain, let us suppose the equation to be against the agricultural country. This would enable the manufacturing country to obtain more for her exports than the price at which she could afford to sell them. It would increase her manufacturing but not her agricultural rate of profit. This would result in a transfer of part of her labor from agriculture to manufactures. If this raised her margin, the price at which she could produce manufactured goods would finally be as great as that she obtained for them, and the advantage gained would no longer be expressed in the equation, but in her margin of cultivation. If, however, her population increased to such extent as to allow of no rise, or only a partial rise, in her margin, it would appear that her rate of manufacturing profit would be permanently greater than her rate of agricultural profit—a manifest absurdity. The two rates can not, of course, vary except for a short time. But the price at which commodities sell is not wholly composed of wages and the profits of fixed capital and active stock. The profit of dead stock is as truly a component of price as any of the others. The element of time that will probably elapse between the production and the sale of goods is always considered by the producer as an element of cost. The higher the price at which he can sell his commodity, other things being equal, the longer he will be content to wait before selling it. When, therefore, the equation of international demand is permanently in favor of a manufacturing nation, the rate of manufacturing profits will, in a short time, be no higher than before, but the amount of dead stock which such nation can accumulate without depressing its industry will be greatly increased. The benefit from the equation being in its favor, will express itself, not in the rate but in the aggregate of manufacturing profits.

I regard this result of the equation of international demand as a very important principle of the science, and for many reasons:

1. It affords a striking verification of the fact herein claimed, that the whole tendency of the equation is to the benefit of manufacturing nations, as it can not be disputed that they are the ones who actually do possess the largest

proportion of dead stock, and even if the reasons for such tendency I have advanced are not valid, it rests with my opponents to find reasons that are, as the result certainly occurs.

2. It points to a deduction that must be made from the benefit accruing under free trade to the productive efficiency of the world—dead stock of itself is of no advantage. Any unnecessary increase in its permanent amount is just so much subtracted from the sum of enjoyed products, and is as much a loss to the world as if it had been consumed by fire. The loss, indeed, is not very great, but it is a real one. But the effect of permanent increase of dead stock is to permanently lower real, though not proportional wages, and it benefits capitalists at the expense of the laborers, a very undesirable result.

3. It affords an economic explanation of the fact that manufacturing are exclusively the lending nations of the world. That they are so has hitherto been attributed to moral causes, and the benefit derived has been regarded as the well-merited reward of superior thrift, abstinence, and industry, whereas it now appears to be a due effect of the laws of international exchange, and a natural and inevitable result of the character of the national occupations rather than of the industry and thriftiness with which such occupations are pursued. The possession of this large amount of dead stock affords at all times to manufacturing communities an available fund for foreign investment. It makes England the store-house and commercial center of the world, and London the capital in which nearly all large loans are raised. Whether or no a proposed investment, promising a profit, shall be made, depends almost wholly on the amount of idle funds belonging to those to whom the investment is proposed.

The known fact that such funds exist is sure to afford to their possessors the choice of all existing opportunities for investment. They are thus enabled not only to select the most promising of such opportunities, but are enabled to very rapidly convert their dead stock into active capital, and thus prevent it from lowering prices and the rate of profit. Accumulation can go on in such nations more rapidly and for a longer time without depressing industrial activity. Any race of men will accumulate more in such circumstances than they would or could in an agricultural status, where comparatively small accumulations so depress the rate of profit that the fund from which accumulations are made is immediately destroyed.*

* This brings us to the last of the counter-forces which check the downward tendency of profit in a country whose capital increases faster than that of its neighbors, and whose profits are therefore nearer to the minimum. This is the perpetual overflow of capital into colonies of foreign countries, to seek higher profits than can be obtained at home. I believe this to have been for many years one of the principal causes by which the decline of profits in England has been arrested. It has a twofold operation: In the first place, it does what a fire, or an inundation, or a commercial crisis would have done; it carries off a part of the increase of capital from which the reduction of profits proceeds. Secondly, the capital so carried off is not lost, but is chiefly employed either in founding colonies, which become large exporters of cheap agricultural produce, or in extending and perhaps improving the agriculture of older communities. It is to the emigration of English capital that we have chiefly to look for keeping up a supply of cheap food and cheap materials of clothing, proportional to the increase of our population; thus enabling an increasing capital to find employment in the country, without reduction of profit in producing manufactured articles with which to pay for this supply of raw produce. Thus, the exportation of capital is an agent of great efficiency in extending the field of employment for that which remains; and it may be said truly that, up to a certain point, the more capital we send away, the more we shall possess and be able to retain at home.

In countries which are further advanced in industry and population, and have therefore a lower rate of profit than others, there is always, long be-

Not only are manufacturing nations, as a result of the character of their industry, afforded opportunities for the accumulation of capital far beyond those of their agricultural neighbors, but they are enabled to usurp for themselves, by means of foreign investment, the few opportunities which are afforded to an agricultural people by the nature of their occupation.

They are enabled to do this by the large amount of funds, available for such investment, which are actually forced into their possession by the tendency of the international equation in their favor, which tendency inevitably increases their dead stock by necessarily increasing the gross amount of their manufacturing profits in proportion to their agricultural profits. As the rate of the one can not but for a very short time exceed that of the other, the two rates can only be brought together by an increase in the amount of capital on which manufacturing profits are paid. Under such circumstances any and every people would accumulate, and it is absurd to praise them for their thrift and abstinence in so doing.

fore the actual minimum is reached, a practical minimum, viz., when profits have fallen so much below what they are elsewhere, that, were they to fall lower, all further accumulations would go abroad. In the present state of the industry of the world, when there is occasion, in any rich and improving country, to take the minimum of profits at all into consideration for practical purposes, it is only this practical minimum that needs be considered. As long as there are old countries where capital increases very rapidly, and new countries where profit is still high, profits in the old countries will not sink to the rate which would put a stop to accumulation. The fall is stopped at the point which sends capital abroad. It is only, however, by improvements in production, and even in the production of things consumed by laborers, that the capital of a country like England is prevented from speedily reaching that degree of lowness of profit which would cause all further savings to be sent to find employment in the colonies, or in foreign countries.

Within the nation itself, the effect of this normally larger amount of dead stock is to lower real wages without any disturbance of proportional. So far as the laborers consume manufactured goods, they pay for them more than they would if the normal amount of dead stock were less. Goods held for a year before they reach the consumer will, in the long run and on the average, cost him about ten per cent more than they otherwise would, and whatever increment of cost is due to this cause operates as a transfer of value, without equivalent, from the consumers to the capitalists, and in so far as such consumers are laborers they suffer a loss of real wages.

The possession of this normally large amount of dead stock is not so much to be considered as itself a tax upon the foreign consumer, as the form in which the tax upon him, caused by the equation of international demand being unfavorable, expresses itself and is gathered by the nation that supplies him with manufactured goods; but it does enable such nation to lay a tribute upon him in the shape of profits and interest upon loans and investments in his country that would else have been made from home accumulations of dead stock, only possible to a manufacturing country. This commercial tribute is very great in amount, and is an addition to the other injuries I have enumerated as resulting to an agricultural nation from an unrestricted intercourse with manufacturing ones.*

* "Before closing this discussion, it is fitting to point out in what manner and degree the preceding conclusions are affected by the existence of international payments *not originating in commerce*, and for which no equivalent in either money or commodities is expected or received; such as a tribute, or remittances of rent to absentee landlords or of interest to foreign creditors, or a government expenditure abroad such as England incurs in the management of some of her colonial dependencies. . . .

No explanation of the fact that manufacturing are the lending and agricultural the borrowing nations of the world, other than that here given, is possible; and the verification of my claim, that the equation of international demand is persistently unfavorable to agricultural nations, is complete.

Fourthly, it aids in the explanation of the observed fact, that, as nations grow in capitalized wealth, there is a tendency for the normal rate of interest—the rate under which capitalists are content to go on accumulating—to be lowered. This tendency is, to a large extent, explicable in the present state of the science, but the principle here enunciated affords an additional reason why the fact occurs: when the amount of dead stock is naturally larger in one country than in another, fresh accumulations of the same amount will form a smaller percentage of the total, and will not affect the rate of profit so much as when added to the accumulations of a nation whose normal amount of dead stock is small. The tendency

"To begin with the case of barter. The supposed annual remittances being made in commodities, and being exports for which there is to be no return, it is no longer requisite that the imports and exports should pay for one another; on the contrary, there must be an annual excess of exports over imports, equal to the value of the remittance. If, before the country became liable to the annual payment, foreign commerce was in its natural state of equilibrium, it will now be necessary, for the purpose of effecting the remittance, that foreign countries should be induced to take a greater quantity of exports than before; which can only be done by offering those exports on cheaper terms, or, in other words, by paying dearer for foreign commodities. The international values will so adjust themselves that either by greater exports, or smaller imports, or both, the requisite excess on the side of exports will be brought about; and this excess will become the permanent state. *The result is, that a country which makes regular payments to foreign countries, besides losing what it pays, loses also something more by the less advantageous terms on which it is forced to exchange its productions for foreign commodities.*"—(Mill's "Principles.")

to accumulate is thereby strengthened, as the risk of its proving entirely useless is lessened, and the same amount of accumulations has less effect in lowering the rate of profit.

The existence of a normally large dead stock is an element of security, and as such affects the desire to accumulate. Capitalists are always better content to invest in securities affording a uniform return than in those affording a variable one, the same, or even somewhat greater, in average amount. They will, therefore, be willing to add more to a normally large dead stock than to a normally small one, even if thereby the rate of profit is somewhat lessened. It is also to be noticed that, if the equation of international demand remains as favorable as before to the manufacturing nation, a lowering of the rate of profit will not reduce the price at which it sells its manufactured goods. Such price depends upon the equation and not upon the rate of profit; but such lowering of the rate of profit, as it can not lessen the aggregate of manufacturing profits, will cause a further increase in the normal amount of dead stock which the manufacturing nation will hold and possess.

I desire to call attention to the explanation, afforded by the principles and tendencies here enunciated, of an otherwise inexplicable historical fact. I refer to the recent and apparently permanent lowering of the rate of interest and profits in the United States. Free-traders are accustomed to assert that our undeniable prosperity under protection is owing to our great natural resources, and is in spite of our fiscal policy and not due to it. They forget that the gain in the efficiency of labor due to free trade is in exact proportion to the agricultural advantages which a nation possesses. The more fertile a nation is, therefore, the greater should be her loss in adopting a protective policy, if they are right as to the effects of free trade and protection upon the distribution of wealth. Protection to manufactures should be more disastrous to us than to nations whose manufacturing industries less need protection. Their explanation is evidently faulty, because our advantage in natural resources can not overbalance our mistaken policy, if the results of that policy are disastrous in proportion to our natural advantages. The fact remains that we have prospered and are prospering, and have succeeded in accumulating vast resources in fixed capital and in active and dead stock, and that the latter species of wealth has increased in greater proportion than the other two. It is this latter fact that explains the permanent lowering of our normal rates of profit and interest. The equation of international demand is no longer against us. Our capital is replacing foreign capital, as is shown by the comparative decrease in our foreign obligations. We yet owe too much abroad, and have as yet only begun to avail ourselves of foreign investment as an avenue for the escape of superabundant means. But we are rapidly paying our debts, and are commencing to invest in other countries, notably in Mexico. By supplying ourselves with manufactured goods we have lessened our demand for foreign goods, and are obtaining those we yet require at cheaper rates and are enjoying a vast increase of capitalized wealth and a very great industrial activity. The efficiency of our labor is undoubtedly somewhat lessened, but that the loss resulting from this has been more than made up to us by the increased aggregate of our profits, by the increase in our productive efficiency through the fuller employment of our labor, and by the adjustment of the equation in our favor, can not be denied as an actually existing fact, and a fact inexplicable on any other theories than those here insisted upon. That much, if not all, of our prosperity has been obtained at the expense of European nations, England especially, is also self-evident. The development of our railroads and water-ways and the discovery of our ability to export live-stock and fresh meat have cheapened agricultural produce to such extent that England can no longer cultivate her poorest lands and pay the same real wages as before. She is, therefore, obliged to throw land out of cultivation, at the very time that she must lower her margin of cultivation, if she would retain her manufacturing supremacy, although the real wages of her laboring classes are already so low that they can not well be further reduced.

A party is arising in England antagonistic to free trade. They demand "fair trade," by which they mean protective duties on imports from those nations who discriminate in their tariffs against the productions of England. How futile, nay disastrous, such a policy will be, can not fail to be appreciated by any one who has followed the argument of this treatise. A nation with a low margin of cultivation can not protect itself against one with a high margin. It is absolutely helpless in the matter of reprisals. Any attempt in that direction only magnifies the injury. The sole advantage that a protective policy can afford is due to its diverting labor from agriculture to manufactures. Protective duties in England, leveled against an agricultural nation with which she trades, can only result in the opposite direction, viz., the diversion of her industry from manufactures to agriculture. This will render her vast capital too great for her needs. It will depress the rate of profit, and lead to a corresponding cessation of industry. It will divert her labor and capital to the employments that will yield the least aggregate returns in wages and profits. England's interests are advanced by free trade. Its general adoption would enable her to appropriate to herself great advantages at the expense of the nations with which she trades, but there will some advantage remain to her by adhering to that policy even when all the agricultural nations, from whom she imports food and raw produce, have excluded her own products. It is this fact that has misled the English school of economists. Their own national affairs are subserved by free trade alone, and afford an apparently complete verification and justification of the doctrine, when the interests of other nations are unconsidered. It was very natural that Mill and Ricardo should have given undue prominence to the facts under their own eyes, and should have neglected facts never presented in English experience; and as natural that American economists and statesmen should have so largely refused to accept their conclusions, despite their not being able to detect the logical flaw in their arguments. The consideration of the tendency in civilized nations for capital to be accumulated faster than it can be utilized, even by a growing population, supplies the logical premise needed, and explains as they never have been explained the economic facts actually existent.

CHAPTER XII.

DISTRIBUTION OF WEALTH IN A PROTECTED NATION.

Having now established on economic principles that the policy of protection may augment the gross revenue of an agricultural nation, the consideration naturally arises as to what effect it will have upon the distribution of such gross revenue between the two great classes of laborers and capitalists. Philanthropic statesmen might well hesitate to adopt a policy which made a nation richer, partly at the expense of its working population. Disparity of individual fortunes is the great curse of modern society, and any advantage gained entirely at the expense of increasing that disparity might well be foregone. There are even some moral and social disadvantages in such increase when it is not obtained at the expense of those who have little, but solely from an augmentation of the gross revenue of society. I at once acknowledge that the policy of protection is open to this latter objection; but it is not, I think, to the former, although that can not be so accurately determined. The bulk of the benefit certainly goes to the increase of profits, but some of it, I think, accrues to the wages-fund. I will here consider the reasons tor this conclusion.

It will be well first to notice a temporary benefit that laborers receive immediately upon the adoption of the policy. The increase of capital necessitated by the diversion of agricultural labor to manufactures raises the rate of profit and lowers proportional wages, and real wages also in so far as the laborer is a consumer of the protected article. This effect upon real wages is, however, more than made up to the laborers as a class by the increased employment that results from such a state of affairs, and this increase of employment lasts until the needed capital is accumulated, when proportional wages advance to the same point as before and real wages also, except as the laborer is a consumer of the protected article, and the amount of employment is the same, other things being equal, as it was originally. How much advantage this temporary increase of the wages-fund will be to the laborer will depend upon the rapidity with which the needed accumulations are made by the capitalists. If all the increased product is converted into capital, the increase of the wages-fund will be exactly equal to the amount of such capital; if only half, the benefit to the laboring class will be twice that amount; and if only one tenth, ten times, subject of course to their loss as consumers of the protected article. As a matter of fact, it may perhaps be estimated that they gain about five times the amount accumulated. This gain is, however, temporary, and of no permanent advantage to the laborer, unless it leads him to advance his standard of living, and it can hardly do this to any appreciable degree. He suffers, eventually, a permanent loss as a consumer of the protected article.

Several benefits obtained by him are, however, to be offset against this loss. And it is hardly possible but that he derives some net benefit from the policy when it really leads to any considerable increase in the national production. Whether he retains the benefit will, of course, depend, as do all other benefits conferred upon him, upon his using it as an enhancement of individual comfort, or as affording him an opportunity of marrying earlier and having a more numerous family.

The diversion of labor from agriculture to manufactures raises in some degree the margin of cultivation, and this can not take place without a rise in real wages. On account of the abundance of our fertile land, this has little influence upon the American margin at the present time, but we are rapidly nearing the point when it will have a very important effect, as most of our best lands are now under some sort of cultivation, and, the moment we commence to take up land at all inferior to our best, we will also feel the beneficial effect of the diversion of our labor from tilling the soil.

Again, whatever increase in their wages skilled artisans receive is an addition to the wages-fund of a very real and important kind, although the benefit goes only to a few of the class, and does not improve the condition of the lowest class of laborers.

The benefit resulting from the increased employment of females and youths is, however, a substantial addition to the incomes of all classes of laborers, and one very considerable in its amount; and one also that assists the class in restraining the instinct that leads to a too rapid increase of population.

There is also probably some benefit derived from the greater diversity in the industries carried on by a protected people. Not only do laborers more easily find the employment for which they are intellectually and physically best fitted, and in which, therefore, labor is less onerous to them and more efficient in production, but the amount of employment is more uniform, as the greater the variety of a nation's pursuits, the less liable are they to be all depressed at the same time, and such variety is in itself an education to the laborer, which spurs him to strive for something better than his present lot.

The possessors of great wealth can not keep its enjoyment wholly to themselves. The beauty of their residences and grounds gives pleasure to the eye of the passer-by as well as to the owners, and the refinements of life with which they surround themselves civilize and refine their menials as well as themselves, though not, of course, to the same degree. Life in a rich community is far more attractive, and a better thing to the laborers, than life in a poor and unkempt land, even if they possess no greater material comforts.

There is also a substantial advantage to the laboring class in living in a community better able to protect itself against its neighbors; and, as Ricardo so conclusively shows, the strength of a nation in war depends not upon its gross but upon its net revenue.

It can not be doubted but that the sum of these advantages more than repays to the laborer the enhanced price of the manufactured commodities he consumes, and even that he can at any time recover by restraining population. To some, though probably a slight degree, he is benefited by protection. If he is not, the moral right of the nation to take fifty cents from his pocket to give a dollar to the capitalist may well be questioned, although, even if that were the result, much might be advanced in defense of such action. But it is not the result, and, although capitalists reap nearly all the benefit of protection, some benefit undoubtedly is obtained by the working classes.

The claim, so blatantly made about election-time, that the purpose of protection is to protect American laborers against the competition of "pauper labor," is, of course, absurd, and can not be too strongly reprobated. To make the laborers understand their true economic position is the first duty of every student and teacher of political and social economy, as it is only when they appreciate the true conditions and limitations of their position that the effort to raise the class by co-operation and the restraint of their instinct to over-populate can be at all effectual. To confuse their minds by false economic ideas is to do them the greatest possible injury.

The gross income of the class of capitalists can not but be increased as the result of a protective policy, even in the rare cases when it entails a positive loss to the laborers. Even then some national advantages result. The refining influences of a wealthy class extend far beyond its own borders, and, as we have seen, the existence of such a class in relatively large proportions adds greatly to the offensive and defensive power of a nation—both most desirable results.

The existence of such a class in larger proportion than would occur under free trade will cause a further augmentation of national wealth that I have not yet noticed. Every increase of capital, needed in industry, being created by the very demand, or rather by the otherwise idle labor, which such demand utilizes, it follows that every diversion of capital to uses which do not affect the rate of profit is an addition to the possible wealth of a people. Such species of wealth is that reserved for prolonged unproductive consumption.

The elegant residences, the public parks and buildings, the museums, the art-galleries, the places of amusement, the sea-side resorts, all these, whatever their expense to individuals, cost the nation nothing but labor that would otherwise be wasted. Such wealth affords no material profit to the community, though it is more or less made to yield a profit to individuals, but this merely affects the distribution of wealth, not its creation; none the less does it yield a revenue, for it gratifies, without its own diminution, the very wants and desires the ultimate satisfaction of which by material products alone gives value to material products themselves. It is the noblest and best wealth a nation can possess, while its cost to it is the least.

But the amount of such wealth will always be regulated more or less closely by the amount of capital which a nation is able to employ productively. Any policy, therefore, that increases such amount, even if it results in no increase of the annual material product, will increase the amount of this species of wealth and the gratifications it annually and for all time yields. Not only will it be increased in proportion to the increase of capitalized wealth, but in a greater proportion, as, the larger the incomes of the rich are, the relatively more of them will they devote to these purposes and to the more refined and æsthetic enjoyments which they afford. No nation can hope to advance beyond its fellows in culture, refinement, and art, and in intellectual and æsthetic attainments, that does not possess a very large proportion of such wealth, and no agricultural nation ever has or ever can possess such wealth in any considerable degree so long as it confines its energies and restricts its capital to the tilling of the soil.

CHAPTER XIII.

RENT.

RICARDO says in his chapter on "Rent," page 40:

"The rise of rent is always the effect of the increasing wealth of the country, and of the difficulty of providing food for its augmented population. It is a symptom but it is never a cause of wealth; for wealth often increases most rapidly while rent is either stationary or even falling. Rent increases most rapidly as the disposable land decreases in its productive powers. Wealth increases most rapidly in those countries where the disposable land is most fertile, where importation is least restricted, and where, through agricultural improvements, productions can be multiplied without any increase in the proportional quantity of labor, and where consequently the progress of rent is slow."

Though in the main I agree with Ricardo in this passage, except, of course, where he affirms that wealth increases most rapidly where importation is least restricted, the meaning would be clearer to me if Ricardo had more accurately defined what he means by wealth. Except as increase of wealth (however defined) increases the demand for native food, it has no effect upon rent, and rent may decline, even when population is increasing, if the nation imports an additional proportion of its food-supply.

Wealth may be intended to mean, and in the quoted passage I take it as meaning, the aggregate wealth of the community, or we may mean, by a wealthy country, one whose wealth is great *per capita* of its population. Or we may not, in using the term, refer to accumulations at all, but to either the gross amount of the annual product or the average amount *per capita*. These four meanings are very different, and the relations of wealth to rent vary greatly according to which of the four meanings we attach to the word. The proper aim of political and social endeavor is to attain wealth in the last meaning I have noted. In that sense an increase of wealth is rather coincident with a fall than with a rise in rentals.

A rise in rent is the cause of an increase of accumulations, because it enables a nation to divert more of its labor to those industries which can utilize accumulations. A rise in rent may therefore be a cause as well as a symptom of wealth.

It is customary to regard rent as a transfer of wealth from the consumer of food to the landlord, and this is true of rent so far as it is due to the natural or acquired fertility of the soil. But it has not been observed—at least I do not remember that it has been observed—that the rent due to propinquity to market is an exception to this, in so far as the consumers of food at an enhanced price are artisans. When this is the case, rent due to propinquity is paid by the consumer of manufactured goods. Food is always somewhat higher in towns and cities than in the country, and, as a consequence of this, lands near towns and cities bring a rental additional to that due to their inherent or acquired fertility exactly, in the long run, equal to such enhanced price due to the saving in cost of carriage. When, therefore, proportional and real wages of artisans and agricultural laborers are the same, the money-wages of the artisans will be higher, and this addition to their money-wages will enhance the price of the goods they manufacture, and will finally be paid by the consumer of those goods. It follows, therefore, that the consumer of any imported manufactured article pays some rent to a foreign landlord, and that a country that protects its manufactures escapes thereby the payment of rent to foreigners.

If the industries that spring up in consequence of protection are concentrated in special localities to the same degree as in the other country, the consumers of goods do not save this rental. If they concentrate in greater degree, they may even pay more than they did before: and, if in lesser degree, less; but, whatever the amount, they pay it to their own countrymen.

The sum total of rentals due to propinquity is considerable, and it is certainly better for a nation to pay it to its own than to foreign landlords; and this effect of protection, as far as it goes, is a valid argument in its favor. The idea here expressed seems to be at the bottom of the popular idea that a home is preferable to a foreign market. That it is so has been instinctively felt, rather than logically appreciated, but a consideration of the fact that rent due to propinquity is an element of the cost of goods shows that the popular idea is right, however illogically held and expressed.

The beneficial influence of protection upon the rentals due to fertility will not, of course, be denied by the most enthusiastic free-traders. A diversion of industry in a protected country from agriculture to manufactures can not but occur, and this forces upon countries with which it trades a corresponding and inverse diversion. Its margin of cultivation is raised, its purely agricultural rents lowered, and rentals due to propinquity increased. This in some degree raises the average remuneration of its labor and lowers its rentals, thus benefiting its laborers at the expense of its landlords. Such benefit, whatever its amount, is in the more even distribution as well as the creation of wealth, bettering the consumer at the landlord's expense, whereas the benefit derived from rentals due to propinquity is an addition to national wealth at the expense of the rentals of the landlords of other nations.

Where the benefits of the concentration of manufactures are an offset or more than an offset to the increase of rentals due to propinquity it may perhaps be technically incorrect to consider such rentals as part of the cost of production of manufactured goods. That, however, does not affect my argument, as in any case they are a source of income, under free trade, to foreigners, which protection enables us to appropriate to ourselves as consumers or landlords.

The rentals yielded by water privileges, while not strictly an element in the cost of production, are likewise an additional income obtained by protection, which formerly pertained to those who supplied us with the protected goods.

While it is immaterial that the above sources of income should be technically considered as an element of cost of production, I must contend that they should be so regarded. They do not, indeed, affect the price at which different manufacturers can afford to produce, any more than a difference in the rental paid by them affects the relative price at which two different farmers can afford to sell the products of their farms; but as a rise in agricultural rents varies the proportion in which raw produce and goods will exchange, so also does a rise in manufacturing rentals increase the exchangeable value of goods as compared with raw produce, and is in every sense an element of their money cost and exchangeable value.

CHAPTER XIV.

COMMERCE.

For the sake of simplicity, I have heretofore confined the discussion to manufacturing and agricultural communities. A few words in reference to the relations of both these to commercial nations is fitting in this place.

The four great divisions of human industry are agriculture, manufacturing, exchanging, and rendering services. The latter does not here demand our consideration, and we have already discussed the first two. Commerce, including by the term exchanges from place to place as well as from producer to consumer, is the third. There is, indeed, no inherent connection between exchanges from place to place and from producer to consumer, but, as a matter of fact, the tendency is more or less strong for the same class of individuals to engage in both employments, though not so strong as for the nations which most largely engage in the carrying-trade to also engage in effecting the exchanges of the goods they carry between different peoples. This tendency in commercial nations is greater if they are also manufacturing communities, as they then possess an additional amount of capital seeking investment, much of which will certainly find its way to employment in effecting international interchange.

In its turn, a large amount of carrying-trade done by a nation reacts to the benefit of its manufacturing industries, as it affords cheaper and quicker transit to its exports and imports. A large merchant marine and, still more, regular steamship-lines to foreign ports, enable a manufacturing community to monopolize markets in which she has no other advantage, or would even be at a disadvantage, if it were not for her better means of communication.

Commerce, as a national industry, possesses advantages over both agriculture and manufacture. Far back as we may go in the history of the world, we invariably find that the nations whose wealth, in proportion to their population, was the greatest were distinctively commercial peoples. Tyre, Sidon, Carthage, Venice, Holland, and finally England, are practical illustrations of the fact asserted. The illustrations given are somewhat complicated by the fact that, owing to the mutual stimulus which the two forms of industry exert, the carrying nations have, to a large extent, been manufacturing ones also; but still the fact is evident that those communities have been the most prosperous who directed the greatest proportion of their industry to commerce.

The main reason of this (those noticed above are only secondary) can be gathered at once from the principles we have been elucidating. Transferring and exchanging commodities utilize more capital in proportion to the labor employed than either branch of production proper. The gross accumulations and the gross return in wages and profits together are larger in it than in any other forms of industry. It possesses, therefore, even greater recommendations as a national employment than manufacturing.

What are the causes which, under free trade, determine whether or not a nation shall engage in this form of industry? Everything, of course, which lowers or raises the price at which she can afford to transport goods from one place to another, or transfer them from the producer to the consumer.

The money cost of transporting goods by any nation will depend mainly upon the lowness of her margin of cultivation; the lower this is, the lower will be the real and money wages of her navigators, and, what is of vastly more importance, the lower will be the money cost of her vessels as far as manufactures enter into such cost. The money cost of raw products will be slightly greater, and that of mineral products will depend upon the fertility of her mines and the lowness of her margin as affecting money-wages. As the cost of putting together is about ninety per cent of the total cost of a vessel, the same merchant marine will be much cheaper in money to nations with low margins—although it will cost them a slightly greater expenditure of labor on account of raw produce forming a small ingredient of the total cost. But, while a commercial country will be favored by a low rate of real wages, she will be benefited by a high rate of proportional wages, as they will not increase the money value of her marine, while they will considerably lessen the amount of the return her capitalists expect, or, in other words, they will be willing to carry for a rate yielding a smaller profit than they would if proportional wages were lower.

But investment in the carrying-trade differs from that in manufactures, not only in the proportion of its amount to the labor employed, and in the proportion which fixed capital bears to circulating, but also in the proportion in which circulating capital will be divided between dead and active stock. The owners of marine investment, unlike manufacturers, can get no profit at all from dead stock in their own business. Profit comes to them in the form of money, and must be invested in fixed capital (new vessels), or outside their business in some other employment, except, indeed, to the extent in which they give credit for freights due, and this can never be considerable. Their active stock is also relatively small, as they employ but few laborers in proportion to the amount of their business.

The other part of commerce, into which they inevitably drift, because in no other way can they so easily get a profit from any dead stock they accumulate—viz., the purchase of foreign produce to hold for, and finally to sell to, the home or foreign consumer—employs, on the other hand, hardly any fixed capital or active stock. Capital so used consists almost wholly of dead stock, but of dead stock that yields a profit.

This hasty explanation of the nature of commerce, inadequate as it is, will suffice for our present purpose, which is to determine the relative advantage or disadvantage of an agricultural nation doing her own carrying, or allowing it to be done for her, as it inevitably must be, if economic laws are allowed full sway. The reader can not fail to see that this advantage or disadvantage can not be ascertained from a comparison of the money cost of doing it herself with what other nations will charge for the service. The comparison must be between what other nations charge and the money cost of the agricultural labor which she must divert to the carrying-trade to do it herself; and that part of the cost, composed of profits, must not be at all considered, as the capital to which such profits will accrue will be an addition to the wealth of the country that will cost nothing except labor that would otherwise be wasted in idleness. It can not be doubted for a moment that even those nations who enjoy the highest margin of cultivation will derive some positive benefit from monopolizing all they can of the carrying-trade of the world, and that any loss in the efficiency of labor they suffer, by diverting it from agriculture to commerce, is several times made up to them in the form of profits.

But how can a nation protect its commerce? It can absolutely prohibit foreigners from engaging in its own coasting-trade—and all or nearly all nations avail themselves of this opportunity, the free-traders as well as the rest, antagonistic as it is to their principles; but it can not prohibit foreign vessels from bringing cargoes to or taking them from its shores, neither can it impose a duty or tonnage upon them for so doing. Retaliation here is possible, as it is not to a manufacturing nation, against whose products an agricultural nation discriminates. If any nation should attempt this, other nations would prohibit or tax her vessels, and a cessation of all trade would result. An agricultural nation finds she can not induce her people to engage in commerce unless they build their own vessels; but they can not do this profitably unless she protects ship-building, and this places her ship-owners at a further disadvantage in their competition with others. In protecting manufactures she controls her own markets, and that is sufficient to allow for a gainful diversion of industry. In commerce also she controls part of her own market, the coasting-trade; but the advantages of engaging in commerce are so great that the market she commands is wholly insufficient for gaining all the advantage possibly derived from commerce: she must, therefore, subsidize—it is her only resource.

Curiously enough, the American people have steadfastly refused to adopt this course—mainly, indeed, for moral reasons, because the corruption and legislative bribery pretty sure to result from such a policy are rightly odious to them. But they subsidize railroads with public lands, and call upon consumers to pay over vast sums to manufacturers, and with manifest benefit to themselves as a people; while they actually force American ships to carry their mails at a positive loss, and refuse subsidies to them in any way or shape, although no conceivable investment of the public money would so augment the total production of the country. Protectionists in principle, we refuse protection to the very industry in which it might yield to us the greatest benefits at the least cost. No wonder our commerce has dwindled away to the vanishing-point, now that we have lost, by the substitution of iron for wood in their construction, our natural advantage in building ships. The loss of our commerce is a very serious drag upon our national prosperity, in every other respect so wisely fostered by our fiscal policy.

England, with the instinctive keenness in regard to her own advantage which she always shows, despite her theories, has pursued a different course, and has heavily subsidized her steamship lines, and none of her free-traders lift an objecting voice to the policy. And yet, if protection is an economic mistake as applied to manufactures, it is equally wrong as applied to commerce. No reason can be given that justifies the one that will not also justify the other, though not, to be sure, to the same degree. Why should the British nation so strenuously endeavor to monopolize this branch of industry, if there are no inherent advantages in one kind of industry over another not expressed by the money cost at which they can be carried on by native or by foreign labor and capital? And if it be once admitted that there are such inherent differences, what becomes of the theory of free trade as applied to the distribution of wealth among nations?

In Book III, chapter xxv, section 5, Mill says:

"It is worth while also to notice another class of small but in this case mostly independent communities, which have supported and enriched themselves almost without any productions of their own (except ships and marine equipments), by a mere carrying-trade, and commerce of entrepot; by buying the produce of one country to sell it at a profit in another. Such were Venice and the Hanse towns. The case of these communities is very simple: they made themselves and their capital the instruments, not of production, but of accomplishing exchanges between the productions of other countries. These exchanges are attended with an advantage to those countries—an increase of the aggregate returns to industry—part of which went to indemnify the agents for the necessary expense of transport, and another part to remunerate the use of their capital and mercantile skill. The countries themselves had not capital disposable for the operation. When the Venetians became the agents of the general commerce of Southern Europe, they had scarcely any competitors; the thing would not have been done at all without them, and there was really no limit to their profits except the limit to what the ignorant feudal nobility could and would give for the unknown luxuries then first presented to their sight. At a later period competition arose, and the profit of this operation, like that of others, became amenable to natural laws. *The carrying-trade was taken up by Holland, a country with productions of its own and a large accumulated capital. The other nations of Europe also had now capital to spare, and were capable of conducting their foreign trade for themselves; but Holland, having from a variety of circumstances a lower rate of profit at home, could afford to carry for other countries at a smaller advance on the original cost of the goods than would have been required by their own capitalists; and Holland, therefore, engrossed the greatest part of the carrying-trade of all those countries which did not keep it to themselves by navigation laws constructed, like those of England, for that express purpose."*

Can one help the deduction, in this short epitome of the transfer of commercial supremacy from nation to nation, that wealth followed commerce as well as commerce wealth, and that England owes her present commercial position very largely to the protective policy of her navigation laws and to her subsidies?

The moral and intellectual advantages to a nation of engaging in commerce are almost if not quite as great as the material, and might well be purchased at a considerable sacrifice of the latter; this, however, is somewhat apart from the strict scientific aspect of the question, and I will merely quote in this connection the following eloquent passage from the "Principles," Book III, chapter xvii, section 5:

"But the economical advantages of commerce are surpassed in importance by those of its effects, which are intellectual and moral. It is hardly possible to overrate the value, in the present low state of human improvement, of placing human beings in contact with persons dissimilar to themselves, and with modes of thought and action unlike those with which they are familiar. Commerce is now what war once was, the principal source of this contact. Commercial adventurers from more advanced countries have generally been the first civilizers of barbarians. And commerce is the purpose of the far greater part of the communication which takes place between civilized nations. Such communication has always been, and is peculiarly in the present age, one of the primary sources of progress. To human beings who, as hitherto educated, can scarcely cultivate even a good quality without running it into a fault, it is indispensable to be perpetually comparing their own notions and customs with the experience and example of persons in different circumstances from themselves; and there is no nation which does not need to borrow from others, not merely particular arts or practices, but essential points of character in which its own type is inferior. Finally, commerce first taught nations to see with good-will the wealth and prosperity of one another. Before, the patriot, unless sufficiently advanced in culture to feel the world his country, wished all countries weak, poor, and ill-governed but his own; he now sees in their wealth and progress a direct source of wealth and progress to his own country. It is commerce which is rapidly rendering war obsolete, by strengthening and multiplying the personal interests which are in natural opposition to it. And it may be said without exaggeration that the great extent and rapid increase of international trade, in being the principal guarantee of the peace of the world, is the great permanent security for the uninterrupted progress of the ideas, the institutions, and the character of the human race."

It is a well-recognized principle that the good policy of any proposed internal improvement does not wholly depend upon its proving a paying investment. We subsidize our railroads, and are proposing to do away with tolls on the Erie Canal; and who can doubt that the latter improvement would have added to the wealth of the nation, even if it had not, as it has, paid its way? Internal commerce has always enjoyed the fostering care of the nation, and no one ventures to doubt the policy, however he may sometimes object to special applications of it. But why should we divert our labor and capital from more efficient to less efficient occupations? For two reasons: First, because great public works are mainly, perhaps eventually wholly, an addition to the possible wealth of the nation—they are equivalent to a destruction of some of its capital, which destruction is very soon made whole by the natural action of human industry and thrift, while the public works remain, and what utilities and enjoyments they do subserve are just so much additional to the real income of the people; and, secondly, because we perceive that the economic effect of no trade or occupation is confined to itself alone, but ramifies through all the arts and employments of the people. But a small portion of the profits we derive from our railroads accrues to their stockholders, or even to their directors. The larger portion of benefit is realized by the travelers, farmers, and merchants, who utilize the facilities they afford. It is safe to say that there is not a bankrupt road in our country that has not been a source of wealth to many times the amount of its own cost. Here we have indicated another advantage of a protective policy. The interplay of benefit between the various occupations and employments of men can not but be greater when their occupations and employments are most diversified. It is of no advantage to a nation of farmers that additional land should be reclaimed, but it is of advantage that machine-shops should be built in their midst, independent of the fact whether such shops can supply them with machinery cheaper than they procured it before; but nothing so reacts upon other trades and employments as the establishment of means of communication. This commerce effects, and thus confers, indirectly through agriculture and manufactures, even greater benefits than it does directly through its own legitimate profits.

CHAPTER XV.

ULTIMATE EFFECTS OF FREE TRADE AND PROTECTION.

I HAVE frankly admitted that free trade increases the total efficiency of the labor of the world, and have only differed from its advocates when they assert that all nations who adopt the policy will derive some portion of the benefit resulting from it. Based on this admission, the objection will be formulated that the views here advanced are immoral, and that no nation has the right to destroy a greater gain to the world to secure a lesser gain to itself. It is to be feared that international morality has not yet reached the stage in which nations will deny themselves a selfish advantage to secure the ultimate good of the race. None the less, however, is it their duty so to do, and the adoption of a protective policy by an agricultural nation is decidedly immoral, if it ultimately lowers the economic and social status of other nations more than it benefits its own. That it does this at the time, can not be denied, but whether it does so ultimately is another question, on the resolution of which the morality or immorality of a protective policy depends.

The ultimate and most desirable economic condition of the globe is that population should be distributed among the different countries in exact proportion to their extent and fertility. The margin of cultivation would then be everywhere the same, and the nature of the industries, in which different people would engage, would be fairly and naturally regulated by the natural advantages of their soil and climate, both as to agriculture and manufactures and the carrying on of commerce. An advanced physical, intellectual, and moral people would still possess advantages over less favored races, but they would be advantages that belonged to it; whereas, at present, the more depressed the state of its laboring population, the greater the advantage possessed by a nation in the most desirable forms of industry. After such ultimate distribution, for any nation to endeavor to appropriate to itself, by a protective policy, more than the share of such occupations that came to it, as the result of an unrestricted commerce, would be entirely without justification, and would necessarily react unfavorably upon itself. Free trade would then secure to each people all that they were entitled to of the fruits of industry. There would be no distinctively agricultural, manufacturing, or commercial nations. Each people would produce for itself everything in the production of which its labor was sufficiently efficient as compared with that of its neighbors, and trade would be entirely in articles in which one nation possessed over others some natural (not artificial) advantage in soil, climate, or the character of its people.

Free trade or protection is the morally best course for nations to pursue, according as either tends to bring about this ultimate and desirable equilibrium of human affairs with the least cost of labor and the least loss of annual production while it is being attained; and, yet more important, that policy is most justifiable under which, when the equilibrium is attained, the uniform and world-wide margin of cultivation will be the highest.

The ultimate equilibrium will be reached in three ways, viz.: by the actual transfer of labor from over-populated to under-populated lands, by the peopling of under-populated communities down to the margin of the over-populated; and, in some degree, it is to be hoped, by the depopulation of over-populated lands. The redistribution of capital will automatically follow that of labor.

Protection supplies an artificial stimulus to all of these methods, while free trade acts as a positive discouragement to any transfer of labor and capital by any of them. The former, therefore, hastens our approach to the ultimate and desirable goal, while the latter greatly retards it. Free trade between an agricultural and a manufacturing nation tends to lower the margin of cultivation in the former and raise it in the latter, without any transfer of population. If population in both remains stationary, the two peoples will finally possess the same margin, except as it is caused to differ by the expense of transporting between them the raw products and such manufactured goods as are consumed by laborers, and that margin will finally settle somewhere between their previous individual margins, and will be nearer to the high margin of the agricultural or the low margin of the manufacturing country, according to the amount of unoccupied fertile land which the agricultural country possesses. If that amount is great, the ultimate margin will be nearly as high as her own previous one; if small, it will be but little above the previous margin of the more sterile land. When this state is reached, further change will not occur. The population of the sterile country will still be very much larger in proportion to its fertility and extent than that of the fertile; and this will necessitate the importation of a large proportion of its food and the exportation of many of the manufactured goods required by the laborers of the fertile land. The ultimate equilibrium attainable under free trade, the average margin being the same, will not, therefore, be as beneficial to the world as the equilibrium that will result from protection, because production in the former case will be saddled with the expense of a much greater expenditure of labor in transferring commodities and raw products from place to place, and there will be a great increase in the amount of dead stock that will necessarily be held and stored up, which not only will cause an unnecessary abstinence in its accumulation, but will cause a larger share of the total product to accrue to the capitalists and a smaller to the laborers in both countries. The final efficiency of labor will not be so great, and the difference will not be a trivial one, but a very substantial deduction from the sum of human enjoyments. But population will not remain stationary. It will increase in both lands. If such increase in both lands presses equally upon the food-supply, the relative margins will not be at all affected. They will both be lowered in an equal degree, and the final equality in margin will never be reached. If, however, as would actually be the case, the population of the fertile increased somewhat more rapidly than that of the sterile land, the two margins would approach each other, but at a declining rate, and the approach would probably cease while they were still a considerable distance apart. Whether any margin of cultivation shall advance or recede depends entirely upon the amount of comforts and subsistence which contents the laboring classes to such degree that they will consent to increase, keep up, or decrease their numbers. It is well settled that any sudden and great increase in real wages will not be wholly expended in an increase of population, and that any sudden and great decrease in wages will to a very considerable degree lessen the number of marriages and births; whereas a very gradual increase in real wages will be mainly or fully lost to the laborers by an increase in their number, while a very gradual decrease in real wages will rarely, if ever, lead to a decrease of population, but will result in the laborers adapting their wants to a lower standard of life.

The first effect of large importations of cheap food will be to considerably raise real wages and the margin of cultivation, and this advantage will not be wholly lost to the laborers because it is a great and sudden advantage. The margin of cultivation in the country from which the food is imported is lowered not only by the increase of its own population, but by the increase of the population of the manufacturing nations to whom it exports food, or rather by the increase of the foreign manufacturing population that depend for their subsistence upon imported food. The first effect of international intercourse to the agricultural nation will, therefore, be to cause a considerable depression of the real wages of its laborers. This depression, being great and sudden, will be resisted by its laboring population refusing to increase at all, or at least as rapidly as before. The first effects, therefore, of free trade are to the restraint of the increase of the joint population of the two countries, and are a check upon the lowering of their average margin of cultivation. The population of the world will not so rapidly increase, and the tendency will be for the population of the sterile country to increase more rapidly than before, and for the population of the fertile country to increase less rapidly; and the latter effect will be somewhat greater in amount than the former. Free trade will confer a benefit upon the world in this respect in so far as it raises the average margin, and a loss in cost of transport and dead stock in so far as it increases or sustains the disparity in population between different lands. At first the gain may overbalance the loss, but finally the loss will be greater than the gain.

As the two margins approach nearer and nearer to each other, the rise in real wages in the sterile and the fall in the fertile country will be more and more gradual. When a point is reached where the laborer in the sterile country uses the whole of the advantage gained in increasing the population, the margin there will become fixed, and the further approach of the two margins will be entirely due to the laborers in the more fertile land consenting to reduce the standard of life at which they will continue to increase their numbers. If they finally refuse to go on increasing before the two margins are brought together, they will no longer approach each other, but will remain permanently different. Under free trade, therefore, the rate of approach will not only be slower and slower as the margins approximate, but the approach itself will wholly cease while they are yet a considerable distance apart. The ultimate equilibrium of margins will not be coincident with uniformity of margin, and agricultural nations can never look forward to the time, if they neglect to adopt a protective policy, when they will not be under some disadvantage in the carrying on of those industries which possess the greatest inherent advantages. They must also deny themselves the moral and political advantages of possessing a relatively large population. The strength and dignity of nations depend largely upon their numbers, and the ultimate distribution of population under free trade can not but lessen the military power of agricultural peoples and their influence in the councils of the world. To attain such power and influence has always been a proper national ambition, the chief aim of diplomacy, and one of the most prominent ends of political action. It is not, indeed, desirable if obtained by a loss of net revenue, but only when the net revenue remains the same or is in some degree increased. But, as I have shown, protection certainly increases the net national revenue of an agricultural nation as well as its population, and under such circumstances the increase of the latter is wholly beneficial, and an addition to the motives for the adoption of a protective policy not heretofore noticed.

The immediate effect of the adoption of a protective policy by an agricultural country is to raise its own margin of cultivation and depress the margin of the manufacturing nations with which it formerly traded. As long as population remains stationary the margins can not approach, nor will they if the increase be mutual and equal, or rather in proportion to the fertility of the unoccupied land. But the higher rate of real wages in the agricultural country will act as a powerful stimulus to population, and the lowered rate in the manufacturing as a powerful deterrent. Nevertheless, the two margins will never become identical if the laborers in the country with the higher margin ultimately refuse to adopt as low a standard of life as the laborers in the manufacturing country. This they would probably do, and, as laborers are more unwilling to descend from, than eager to rise above, their previous standard, the ultimate equilibrium of margin will more nearly approach uniformity than under free trade.

But the difference in margins will tend to adjust the

population in another way. The greater it is, the greater stimulus it will afford to emigration. A protected country will inevitably draw to its shores a greater number of immigrants than before, not only because it can offer them a substantial increase in their real wages, but because it can offer them a greater variety of employment. This will also enable it to attract a better class of workmen, those accustomed to earn and receive a higher than the average wages. A skilled artisan who emigrates to an unprotected country can only expect to be employed there as a common laborer. The inducement to leave his native land is very much lessened, and he will not come at all unless the wages of common labor in such country are greater than the wages which his skilled labor commands in his own.

Protection no more than free trade secures, when the final equilibrium is reached, a uniform and universal margin of cultivation, and does not therefore finally affect a distribution of population among nations in exact proportion to their extent and fertility, but it does this latter to a much greater degree than free trade, and does it more quickly. When the margins have approached each other to the same degree as under free trade, the disparity in population will not indeed be entirely overcome, but it will be very much less than if a protective policy had not been adopted. Under protection the disparity will be in exact or nearly exact proportion to the difference in the margins. Under free trade this will be only true of the agricultural population. The sterile and over-populated country will have in proportion to its fertility, besides its somewhat greater agricultural population, a very much larger manufacturing population. This will involve in the ultimate state a very great increase in the cost of carriage between countries, and is far from being to the world as beneficial as the more equal distribution of population effected by protection. Protection will not, indeed, wholly remove in the ultimate state the relative disadvantage of agricultural nations in engaging in the most advantageous employments, but it will lessen it more than the policy of free trade.

The ultimate state under protection is, therefore, in several ways more desirable than that arrived at under free trade, and will be sooner reached. The price paid for this result is a present loss in the efficiency of the labor of the world. Whether the result is fully worth the price can not perhaps well be determined, but that it is worth a large part of it can not surely be denied. To whatever extent it is an equivalent, it morally justifies the adoption of the policy by agricultural nations. It must be noticed, also, that the loss in efficiency is a constantly declining one, and grows less exactly in proportion to the more equal distribution of population. And where such distribution is fully effected, the loss is turned into a gain, the efficiency of labor being then greater by whatever saving is effected in cost of carriage and dead stock.

We have yet to consider whether the ultimate uniform or average margin of cultivation will be higher or lower if agricultural nations generally adopt the policy of protection. Although the determination of this point would more powerfully affect our decision as to the morality of protection than any of the results we have considered, I do not see how it can be arrived at. Whether the margin shall be high or low depends mainly upon moral and social causes, and is only dependent upon economic causes in so far as they act upon the moral and intellectual status of the population. I confess myself unable to see any effect upon the morality or intelligence of the laboring classes of the world at large that can with certainty or even probability be attributed to either free trade or protection, except that the latter causes those nations in which the position of the laborer is the highest to become wealthier and more powerful, while the former gives power and influence to those in which the position of the laborer is the lowest. This effect, however, I can not but regard as very important, and practically decisive of the question at issue.

The authority of Mill in the following passage would seem to be in favor of the morality of protection, judged by the standards here set forth. He says, in Book III, chapter xvii, section 3:

> "It is possible that one of the two countries may be altogether inferior to the other in productive capacities, and that its labor and capital could be employed to greatest advantage by being removed bodily to the other. The labor and capital which have been sunk in rendering Holland habitable, would have produced a much greater return if transported to America or Ireland. The produce of the whole world would be greater, or the labor less, than it is, if everything were produced where there is the greatest absolute facility for its production. But nations do not, at least in modern times, emigrate *en masse;* and while the labor and capital of a country remain in the country, they are most beneficially employed in producing, for foreign markets as well as for its own, the things in which it lies under the least disadvantage, if there be none in which it possesses an advantage."

Ricardo also, in his chapter on "Foreign Trades," page 77, takes the same view. Of course, neither of them recognize or could well recognize, holding the views they did as to the nature of capital, that protection tended to the readjustment of labor and capital they recognized as most beneficial. They both reason as if labor and capital, especially the latter, could only be transferred by actual emigration, whereas this operates but to a very limited extent. The real and effectual method of transfer from one nation to another is, as to capital, its decline in one country and increase in another, due to a change in their relative rate of profit, and as to labor the restraint or stimulus to population due to a change in their relative margin of cultivation. They seem to regard both capital and population, once acquired, in the light of natural instead of artificial advantages, and never to have contemplated their readjustments as possible in the manner I have indicated, although that is the manner by which the readjustment is mainly effected.

Emigration, even when the emigrant is empty-handed, causes of itself a transfer of capital from the mother to the adopted country. By lessening the supply of labor it raises proportional wages and lessens production and accumulation in the former, and by increasing the supply of labor it produces the contrary effect in the latter. It makes but little, and that only a temporary difference, whether or no immigrants bring with them the capital necessary to their employment. Their presence alone, whatever their poverty, allows of the creation of just the amount of capital which their labor can utilize, and very soon their adopted country is as rich as economic law allows, and she can be no richer, however much wealth is transferred bodily to her from other lands.

CHAPTER XVI.

TAXATION.

The recognition of the tendency of capital to outstrip population, not only affords a principle by which intercourse with foreign nations should be regulated, but also assists in determining the policy that should be pursued in the internal affairs of a people, especially in so far as such internal affairs relate to taxation. If there is a tendency for accumulation, carried beyond a certain and frequently recurring point, to lessen production, the effect of such tendency can certainly be largely counteracted by a judicious fiscal system. This being so, the principle that as far as possible taxes should come from accumulations, and not from wages, profits, or unproductive consumption, is surely as important as any of the justly celebrated principles enunciated by Adam Smith.

All direct taxation of profits as such, or indirect through wages or upon unproductive consumption, to such degree or in such manner as leads to a decrease in the value unproductively consumed by the government and the community combined, lessens the productive capacity of the nation, it may be, by an amount far greater than that of the tax itself. It has hitherto been held that taxes that lowered the rate of profit acted injuriously only as they lessened the amount of the sum from which accumulations could continue to be made. But we have seen that such accumulations would have gone first to increase the dead stock or idle capital, and that the amount of active stock or utilized capital, other things being equal, varies inversely with the amount of dead stock. This effect, therefore, would lead to an increased rather than a decreased annual production. Such a tax is, in fact, rarely or never followed by an increased production, but it is not because of the consequent decrease of capital stock, active and passive together, but because the decrease in the rate of profit has lessened the amount of capital that can be productively employed. It has decreased the normal ratio of active to dead stock, and the failure to accumulate further only partially counteracts the consequent disproportion between them.

In countries where population tends to outstrip capital, a tax on profits does, indeed, discourage production, as well by the consequent decrease in capital as by the accompanying decrease in the rate of profit; but where the tendency is the other way, the first result, instead of intensifying, counteracts the second, and finally readjusts the equilibrium of active to dead stock to a new and lower ratio.

Taxes, on the other hand, that are paid wholly from funds that would otherwise have been added to capital, provided, of course, they are not so great as to cause the increase of capital to lag behind that of population, are met entirely by an increase of production. If such taxes had not been levied, the same amount of production might have gone on for a while; but the resulting accumulations would have been added to dead stock, and been followed very soon by a decrease in the amount of stock productively employed, and the total production would have eventually been lessened. The normal ratio between dead and active stock can only be readjusted by a decrease of production, or by an increase of unproductive consumption. A tax drawn wholly from accumulations, being really an increase of unproductive consumption, adjusts it in the latter, and much the more advantageous, way. When such a tax is wisely expended it is an unmixed advantage to the nation, and even when unwisely used it is of no positive disadvantage.

We are entitled, then, to lay it down, not only as a, but as the, fundamental principle of taxation, that it should come as far as possible from funds that would otherwise be added to capital; but in effecting this it must be done without affecting the *rate* of profit, as the effect of lowering that will overbalance the advantage of lessening accumulations.

To reach this fund, from which taxation should wholly come, is a very difficult matter, because every individual on whom taxation falls seeks to meet it, not from the funds he is accustomed or desirous of adding to his capital, but from those he devotes to unproductive consumption. Personal interests here are in direct conflict with social, with the result that a theoretically perfect system of taxation is impossible of attainment, especially as the tax which comes nearest in principle to the correct one, and from which any considerable revenue can be raised, is open to very serious moral objections, and to most minds seems to discriminate very unjustly between individuals. I refer, of course, to a graduated income-tax. A tax upon incomes strictly proportional is a tax upon profits, and therefore objectionable. In so far as it is a tax upon wages, unless indeed they are exceptionally high, it is, of course, transferred eventually to profits, and can not but result in a decrease of production; but, where small incomes are wholly exempt, and moderate incomes but lightly taxed, the weight of the tax falls almost wholly upon the accumulating class, and that very nearly in proportion to their ability and willingness to accumulate. This has hitherto been advanced as a fatal objection to such a tax both economically and morally. We have seen that economically it is not unwise, but, on the contrary, most beneficial to the interests of the community at large, and it is certainly just and right that the class whose advancement of their individual interest most conflicts with the interests of society should be called upon to bear very much more of the public burdens than would otherwise fall to them, especially when their so doing will partially, and may even wholly, obliterate the injurious effects to others of their hitherto too rapid growth in wealth, and that without any diminution, but rather to the increase, of their wealth as a class, although the distribution of their wealth among themselves will be affected. Anything that increases the average annual production increases in some proportion the capital that can be utilized, and consequently the amount that can be accumulated; and that capital should be more equally distributed has long been recognized as a desirable social change. The objections to a graduated income-tax are therefore reduced solely to its inquisitorial nature, and to the deceit and perjury consequent upon the conflict of individual and social interests. Great as these objections are, they do not seem insuperable when the economic action of such a tax is considered.

A legacy-tax, graduated or not, but better if graduated, also meets the conditions of the principle that taxation should be drawn from accumulations, and is not open to the same moral objections. A tax upon gifts above a certain amount would not only be economically advisable, but probably necessary, to prevent evasions of taxes upon legacies and inheritances, and also, perhaps, upon income.

In the following passage from Mill, Book V, chapter ii, section 7, it would certainly seem that he fully indorses the views here advanced. I am unable to put any construction on his language other than that he means to assert that, in England at least, capital so presses upon population that taxes on capital are fully paid by a saving of the waste of capital that would else occur; nor am I able to imagine any more complete admission than this, that over-accumulation is not only possible, but an event of frequent and periodical occurrence, in civilized communities. Mill, indeed, did not perceive that over-accumulations are not only necessarily wasted, but that they involve a partial cessation of industry while such waste is taking place and until it is accomplished. Other than this last particular his views certainly seem to coincide with mine. The passage reads:

"All taxes, therefore, are in some sense partly paid out of capital; and in a poor country it is impossible to impose any tax which will not impede the increase of the national wealth. But in a country where capital abounds and the spirit of accumulation is strong, this effect of taxation is scarcely felt. Capital having reached the stage in which, were it not for a perpetual succession of improvements in production, any further increase would soon be stopped, and having so strong a tendency even to outrun those improvements, that profits are only kept above the minimum by emigration of capital, or by a periodical sweep called a commercial crisis—to take from capital by taxation what emigration would remove or a commercial crisis destroy, is only to do what either of those causes would have done, namely, to make a clear space for further saving.

"I can not, therefore, attach any importance, in a wealthy country, to the objection made against taxes on legacies and inheritances, that they are taxes on capital. It is perfectly true that they are so. As Ricardo observes, if £100 are taken from any one in a tax on houses or on wine, he will probably save it, or a part of it, by living in a cheaper house, consuming less wine, or retrenching from some other of his expenses; but if the same sum be taken from him because he has received a legacy of £1,000, he considers the legacy as only £900, and feels no more inducement than at any other time (probably feels rather less inducement) to economize in his expenditure. The tax, therefore, is wholly paid out of capital; and there are countries in which this would be a serious objection. But, in the first place, the argument can not apply to any country which has a national debt, and devotes any portion of revenue to paying it off; since the produce of the tax, thus applied, still remains capital, and is merely transferred from the tax-payer to the fund-holder. But the objection is never applicable in a country which increases rapidly in wealth. The amount which would be derived, even from a very high legacy-duty in each year, is but a small fraction of the annual increase of capital in such a country; and its abstraction would but make room for saving to an equivalent amount; while the effect of not taking it, is to prevent that amount of saving, or cause the savings, when made, to be sent abroad for investment. A country which, like England, accumulates capital not only for itself but for half the world, may be said to defray the whole of its public expenses from its overflowings; and its wealth is probably at this moment as great as if it had no taxes at all. What its taxes really do is to subtract from its means not of production but of enjoyment; since whatever any one pays in taxes he could, if it were not taken for that purpose, employ in indulging his ease or in gratifying some want or taste which at present remains unsatisfied."

If Mill had borne in mind and fully considered the above words and all that they imply, he could hardly have expressed himself as he does later on in Book V, chapter ii, section 3, in which he says:

"Both in England and on the Continent a graduated property-tax has been advocated on the avowed ground that the state should use the instrument of taxation as a means of mitigating the inequalities of wealth. I am as desirous as any one that means should be taken to diminish those inequalities, but not so as to relieve the prodigal at the expense of the prudent. *To tax the larger incomes at a higher percentage than the smaller, is to lay a tax on industry and economy; to impose a penalty on people for having worked harder and saved more than their neighbors. It is not the fortunes which are earned, but those which are unearned, that it is for the public good to place under limitation. A just and wise legislation would abstain from holding out motives for dissipating rather than saving the earnings of honest exertion.* Its impartiality between competitors would consist in endeavoring that they should all start fair, and not in hanging a weight upon the swift to diminish the distance between them and the slow. Many, indeed, fail with greater efforts than those with which others succeed, not from difference of merits but difference of opportunities; but if all were done which it would be in the power of a good government to do, by instruction and by legislation, to diminish this inequality of opportunities, the difference of fortune arising from people's own earnings could not justly give umbrage. With respect to the large fortunes acquired by gift or inheritance, the power of bequeathing is one of those privileges of propercy which are fit subjects for regulation on grounds of general expediency; and I have already suggested, as a possible mode of restraining the accumulation of large fortunes in the hands of those who have not earned them by exertion, a limitation of the amount which any one person should be permitted to acquire by gift, bequest, or inheritance. Apart from this, and from the proposal of Bentham (also discussed in a former chapter),* that collateral inheritance in case of intestacy should cease and the property escheat to the state, I conceive that inheritances and legacies, exceeding a certain amount, are highly proper subjects for taxation, and that the revenue from them should be as great as it can be made without giving rise to evasions, by donation during life or concealment of property such as it would be impossible adequately to check. The principle of graduation (as it is called), that is, of levying a larger percentage on a larger sum, though its application to general taxation would be in my opinion objectionable, seems to me both just and expedient as applied to legacy and inheritance duties."

* *Supra*, Book II, chapter ii.

In one passage he objects to a tax, in that it tends to discourage accumulation; and in the other he rebuts the same objection against another tax, on the ground that such accumulations will inevitably be wasted. But there are not the moral objections he urges to a graduated tax upon property and incomes, or upon inheritances, legacies, and gifts. The tendency of such taxes is to discourage accumulation, which, if not carried too far, is an unmixed benefit. Their imposition tends not only to a more equal distribution of wealth, but also to the prolongation of the periods of large productiveness. As great accumulations take away from the poorer members of a community something of their ability to themselves accumulate, it certainly seems just that those whom society protects in inflicting an injury upon itself should be called upon to support more than their share, if not all, of the public burdens. There is one peculiar advantage possessed by such a tax which should be noticed, viz., that the community, including those who pay it, will be richer instead of poorer by it, even if the proceeds of the tax be wasted. The increase of industry to which it leads will add more to the general income than the tax itself will subtract from it, because only a part of such increased production will be added to savings, while the tax is wholly a deduction from past accumulations. The conditions, therefore, favorable to a large production will be prolonged.

In his discussion of the income-tax, which follows the passage we have quoted, Mill argues in favor of exempting such a proportion of life-incomes from taxation as would probably be saved. This would indeed be a benefit to the families of annuitants, as it would help to provide for them after the death of the annuitant, but its effect upon accumulation would be against the interest of the public, instead of in favor of it, as Mill supposes.

Taxes upon rental also meet economic conditions, as the unproductive consumption of the government exactly takes the place of the lessened unproductive consumption of the landlords, and therefore, while lessening accumulation, they do not otherwise affect the rate of profit. Mr. Henry George seems to think that a sum could be derived from this source sufficient, not only to meet all the expenses of government, but to allow a vastly increased expenditure by government for social improvement. That a large sum could be so derived admits of no doubt, but that Mr. George considerably exaggerates the amount is also evident. Economic rent is but a small portion of what is ordinarily called rent. A tax upon aggregate rent would be mainly a tax upon profits, and would discourage agricultural and urban improvement, nor do I understand Mr. George to advocate it; but the rent of agricultural land is very largely composed of the profits due to the improvements upon it. It is only of town-lots and villa-sites that economic rent furnishes a large proportion of the rental in the popular sense of the word. If, however, the whole of economic rents were reappropriated by society, it would undoubtedly afford a revenue, which would obviate any necessity of taxing profits in any way or shape, and the economic advantages resulting from this would be very great. I agree with Mr. George that society would be justified in resuming its right to the entire economic rental of its land, but can not regard his proposal to do so immediately and without compensation as anything but the most arbitrary confiscation. Society has parted with its rights in the premises for valuable though inadequate compensation, and though we may allow that one generation can not grant rights of this character belonging to its successors, it certainly can, if it chooses, part with its own. Immediate resumption of economic rentals without full compensation would therefore be most unjust, and the violation of an implied contract. More, however, can be said in favor of a gradual resumption without compensation. The past and the present rights are gone. However inadequate the price, the bargain has been made and must be adhered to, but the grant may be held void as to the generation coming into being, and there would be no injustice in a law resuming the proprietary right to the rental of each future year, in proportion to the ratio of the inhabitants of the country born after its passage to those born before. Such a gradual resumption would work neither hardship nor injustice, and would in time attain for us all the advantages that a sudden and unjust resumption could do, and that without the shock to society that would follow a sudden resumption with or without compensation.

Mr. George entirely miscalculates the effect upon "progress and poverty" that would follow the resumption of economic rent by the government. It would make no difference in the price of food or of manufactured articles whether the farmer and the manufacturer paid the rental to the government, to the landlords, or to themselves as landlords. The sole relief that would accrue would be the consequent relief from other taxation. But the laborer is not, indeed can not be, taxed; at first, probably, he would reap some benefit as a consumer in so far as taxation is an element of cost; but as soon as population had increased, his real wages would be the same as before, and the whole benefit derived from the decrease of other taxation would accrue to his employers by enabling them to utilize a larger amount of capital. The final result would simply be a transfer from landlords to capitalists, and an increase in the inequality of individual fortunes.

The position of the laborer can be permanently improved in but two ways: first and mainly, by his refraining from increasing population; and, secondly, by such a readjustment of social forces as shall result in his *steadier* and more *efficient* employment.

While to some extent agreeing with Mr. George, I can not therefore look hopefully upon his proposed expedient for ameliorating the condition of laborers. I do not, however, despair of their future state, because I see in co-operation the solution, and the only final solution, of the conflict between labor and capital. While its immediate success can not be expected, because it presupposes an intelligence and morality not yet attained by our lower classes, its gradual adoption is certain to take place, small as is the foothold it has yet obtained, because it contains within itself an educative principle that will eventually supply the needed intelligence and morality.

Taxes on necessaries can not but lower the rate of profit, and are always unwise. Taxes on luxuries may or may not lower the rate of profit. If they lead to an increase in the value of what is unproductively consumed, they will raise and sustain the rate, and will act beneficially. If they lead to a decrease of unproductive consumption, they will decrease the rate of profit, and will eventually lessen industrial activity. When they are laid on a few articles and are excessive in amount, they may sometimes do the latter, but when laid upon many articles their operation is similar to that of a graduated income-tax. As the proportion of income spent in luxuries is largest, as a general rule, in large incomes, such taxes curtail the amount of the funds from which accumulations are ordinarily made, and lead to an increase of industrial activity; but they are much inferior in their action to a graduated income-tax, because they do not operate heavily enough against the large incomes, and because many of the rich escape their due proportion of them by unduly curtailing their expenditure. These are pre-eminently the accumulating class, and the one that the good of society demands should be most heavily taxed. But, just in proportion as they monopolize the avenues of investment to the exclusion of their fellow-citizens, for which privilege they should certainly be made to pay, do they escape the taxes upon luxuries. The special advantage of taxing luxuries is that, as in the main, luxurious expenditure increases in greater proportion than income, it is really a slightly graduated tax upon incomes. If such taxes are relied upon, a somewhat heavier tax, according to our principles, should be laid upon the excess of income above expenditure.

Perhaps no better test of the correctness of the principles advocated in this work, as compared with Mill's views, can be found than the effect produced upon a nation's industry by its engaging in war, with the consequent increase in loans and taxes.

To obtain Mill's views I make the following extract from Book V, chapter vii, section 1:

"SECTION 1. The question must now be considered how far it is right or expedient to raise money for the purposes of government, not by laying on taxes to the amount required, but by taking a portion of the capital of the country in the form of a loan and charging the public revenue with only the interest. Nothing need be said about providing for temporal wants by taking up money; for instance, by an issue of exchequer bills, destined to be paid off at farthest in a year or two, from the proceeds of the existing taxes. This is a convenient expedient, and, when the government does not possess a treasure or hoard, is often a necessary one, on the occurrence of extraordinary expenses, or of a temporary failure in the ordinary sources of revenue. What we have to discuss is the propriety of contracting a national debt of a permanent character; defraying the expenses of a war or of any season of difficulty by loans, to be redeemed either very gradually and at a distant period, or not at all.

"This question has already been touched upon in the first book.* We remarked that if the capital taken in loans is abstracted from funds either engaged in production or *destined to be employed in it*, their diversion from that purpose is equivalent to taking the amount from the wages of the laboring classes. Borrowing, in this case, is not a substitute for raising the supplies within the year. *A government which borrows does actually take the amount within the year, and that too by a tax exclusively on the laboring classes—than which it could have done nothing worse if it had supplied its wants by avowed taxation; and in that case the transaction and its evils would have ended with the emergency; while by the circuitous mode adopted the value exacted from the laborers is gained, not by the state, but by the employers of labor*, the state remaining charged with the debt besides, and with its interests in perpetuity. The system of public loans, in such circumstances, may be pronounced the very worst which, in the present state of civilization, is still included in the catalogue of financial expedients.

"We, however, remarked that there are other circumstances in which loans are not chargeable with these pernicious consequences, namely: first, when what is borrowed is foreign capital, the overflowings of the general accumulations of the world; or, secondly, when it is capital which either would not have been saved at all unless this mode of investment had been open to it, or after being saved would have been wasted in unproductive enterprises or sent to seek employment in foreign countries. When the progress of accumulation has reduced profits either to the ultimate or to the practical minimum—to the rate, less than which would either put a stop to the increase of capital, or send the whole of the new accu-

* *Supra*, p. 49.

mulations abroad—government may annually intercept these new accumulations without trenching on the employment or wages of the laboring classes in the country itself, or perhaps in any other country. To this extent, therefore, the loan system may be carried without being liable to the utter and peremptory condemnation which is due to it when it overpasses this limit. What is wanted is an index to determine whether, in any given series of years, as during the last great war, for example, the limit has been exceeded or not."

We have nothing to do here with the question as to the advisability of loans, but with the assertion, in the sentences italicized, that such loans are entirely at the expense of the laboring class, if they raise the rate of profit and depress proportional wages. According to Mill, when such loans are made, they should be followed by some cessation of industry. Is this, in fact, what occurs? Can it be denied that the laboring class is especially prosperous under such circumstances? Mill himself does not attempt to deny it, but endeavors to explain it away in the succeeding paragraph. He says:

"*Such an index exists, at once a certain and obvious one. Did the government by its loan operations augment the rate of interest?* If it only opened a channel for capital which would not otherwise have been accumulated, or which, if accumulated, would not have been employed within the country, this implies that the capital which the government took and expended could not have found employment at the existing rate of interest. So long as the loans do no more than absorb this surplus, they prevent any tendency to a fall of the rate of interest, but they can not occasion any rise. *When they do raise the rate of interest, as they did in a most extraordinary degree during the French war, this is positive proof that the government is a competitor for capital with the ordinary channels of productive investment, and is carrying off not merely funds which would not, but funds which would have found productive employment within the country. To the full extent, therefore, to which the loans of government during the war caused the rate of interest to exceed what it was before, and what it has been since, those loans are charge-*

able with all the evils which have been described. If it be objected that interest only rose because profits rose, I reply that this does not weaken but strengthens the argument. If the government loans produce the rise of profits by the great amount of capital which they absorb, by what means can they have had this effect unless by lowering the wages of labor? It will perhaps be said that what kept profits high during the war was not the drafts made on the national capital by the loans, but the rapid progress of industrial improvements. This, in a great measure, was the fact, and it no doubt alleviated the hardship to the laboring classes, and made the financial system which was pursued less actively mischievous, but not less contrary to principle. These very improvements in industry made room for a large amount of capital; and the government, by draining away a great part of the annual accumulations, did not indeed prevent that capital from existing ultimately (for it started into existence with great rapidity after peace), but prevented it from existing at the time, and subtracted just so much while the war lasted from distribution among productive laborers. If the government had abstained from taking this capital by loan, and had allowed it to reach the laborers, but had raised the supplies which it required by a direct tax on the laboring classes, it would have produced (in every respect but the expense and inconvenience of collecting the tax) the very same economical effects which it did produce, except that we should not now have had the debt. The course it actually took was therefore worse than the very worst mode which it could possibly have adopted of raising the supplies within the year; and the only excuse or justification which it admits of (so far as that excuse could be truly pleaded) was hard necessity—the impossibility of raising so enormous an annual sum by taxation, without resorting to taxes which, from their odiousness or from the facility of evasion, it would have been found impracticable to impose."

This explanation, which, of course, I do not at all allow to be a valid one, at the best is only that of one particular occurrence of the fact so antagonistic to his theories. How lame and impotent it is, is apparent when it is remembered that an increase of industrial activity always occurs in nations while at war; and the higher the war expenditures and loans force the rate of interest and of profit, provided, of course, that the security of capital is not imperiled by invasion, the greater the industrial activity whenever the drain of capital is greater than the drain of labor to the army. When the drain of the latter is the greater, the contrary effect always has been produced.

The reasoning is utterly oblivious of the fact that the benefit which the laboring class receives from capital is solely from such portion of the gross capital as is actively employed in production. Dead stock can not be converted into wages until it becomes active, and the larger the amount of dead stock the less the temptation to capitalists to employ it productively. The drain upon dead stock made by the government loans in time of war, even when it is far greater than what would carry off the sums that would otherwise be loaned abroad or consumed in speculation, is of great and immediate advantage to the laborers. Productive consumption is vastly increased, and the wages-fund consequently enlarged. There is a fall of proportional wages, but the fall of proportional wages is more than made up to the laborers by more of them being kept busy. This accounts for what has hitherto been somewhat of a puzzle to economists, the exceptional prosperity of a country engaged in war, and the continuance of that prosperity after the war is closed, if the increased industry has not already repaired the breaches which the war expenditure has made in capital. The advantage to labor would be greater if it were not for the drain upon their numbers by enlistment and draft. This operates as a counterbalance to the drain of capital, and if it equals or exceeds it, either no increase or a decrease of industrial activity will ensue, because it will raise wages and lessen the wages-fund.

CHAPTER XVII.

SOME OTHER EFFECTS OF THE LAW.

THE recognition that capital is limited by population and tends constantly to overpass such limit, will go far toward the solution of many other eagerly-discussed problems.

The effect of the creation, the funding, and the repayment of national indebtedness upon production and distribution, is such a problem. Some have gone so far as to assert a national debt to be a national blessing; and to a certain degree the assertion can be sustained. Besides the national securities being so readily negotiable and so satisfactory as collaterals, that their presence materially aids the efficiency of the credit system, it may also be affirmed of national indebtedness that, in so far as its creation is at the expense of superfluous capital—i. e., in so far as it only appropriates funds whose existence would discourage future production—it acts as a stimulus to industry, temporary to be sure, but effective and beneficial as long as it lasts. This remark, however, only applies to such part of the debt as is due to the individuals composing the indebted nation. What a government borrows of foreigners fails to deplete its own dead stock, and consequently to augment its own rate of profit and its industrial activity. Such loans are not even of temporary benefit to industry, unless they are employed productively for wise projects, which would not else have been undertaken at all. They are only justifiable to nations whose existence is threatened, or who are in need of great internal improvements that they lack means to provide for themselves. But so far as a nation's loans are drawn from the funds of its own citizens, their first effect is to increase both the rate and the sum total of profits, and to increase, though in a somewhat less degree, the total of the wages-fund and the rate of real wages.

After the loans are completed and expended, and after capital has again adjusted itself to population, this beneficial effect ceases, and national indebtedness becomes more or less detrimental to production. In so far as the consequent taxation adds to the cost of production, it lessens the benefit of foreign trade. Though this is a serious loss, it is so well recognized a result of national indebtedness that it does not demand from us a notice adequate to its importanace, and its consideration need not further detain us.

Whatever of the proceeds of taxation is returned in the form of interest to its own citizens, does not, of course, affect the net income of the nation, and, except as it stimulates accumulation, has no influence upon production. Whatever is so paid to foreigners is, on the other hand, altogether at the expense of the net national income, and can not but result in a total loss, except as it is counterbalanced by benefits still enjoyed through the employment of the original loan in projects for which the national capital was insufficient. Whatever this loss of net income, the gross annual product of the indebted nation need not be decreased, provided the consequent loss of revenue is not so great as to forbid the accumulations necessary for its wages-fund and fixed capital. When payments of interest or other remittances to foreigners (such, for instance, as tribute or for funds expended by absentees) are so great, as is the case with Ireland, India, and a few other unfortunate lands, that they cause population to press upon capital, not only is the net revenue of such a people reduced, but the gross product as well.

That foreign indebtedness need not decrease the gross product of a nation is, however, only true of its amount, and not of its value. As has been ably shown by Mill, the equation of international demand is always disastrously affected, to a creditor nation, by its remittances on account of absentees, tribute, loans, interest, or profits. The value of its gross product can not but diminish, although its amount may not do so as long as its population remains the same, and its capital is not too much depleted or supplanted. But the effect of this national loss in depressing real wages, by lessening the stimulus to population, will finally lead to a decrease of the gross product also, at least relatively to what it might have been, if such foreign indebtedness had never been incurred.

Repayment of the principal of its national debt to its own citizens is wholly an addition to the capital of the country, unless the necessary funds are derived from a tax upon capital. In so far as it adds to capital, it, of course, disturbs its ratio to population, and tends to bring about, sooner than it would otherwise occur, the period of industrial stagnation that inevitably results from over-accumulation. National net income and gross product are both diminished by the process. When such repayment is made to foreigners, production is not disturbed (and, in so far as the taxation, from which the funds so expended are derived, depletes the national capital, production is even increased), but as the equation of international demand is injuriously affected, its value, though not necessarily its amount, is lessened.

All of the above remarks apply as well to private as to public foreign indebtedness, except that private borrowing abroad, being always for productive purposes, affects the normal ratio of national capital to population, by allowing foreign capital to monopolize the avenues for investment, by which alone home accumulations can be utilized or retained. This not only hastens the period when capital will be found to have exceeded its limits, and thus lessens industrial activity and production, but it also allows foreigners to possess themselves of profits that would elsewise have very soon accrued to the future savings of home capitalists.

There is no economic fallacy more firmly fixed in the popular mind than the belief that a nation derives advantage from borrowing of its neighbors. We now see how insidious and disastrous such a policy really is, and that whatever interest and profits are paid on such loans are purely and simply gifts, in all cases where a tendency exists in the indebted nation for capital to increase more rapidly than population. Indeed, such interest and profits are far from expressing the real amount of such gifts —a sum, almost as great, must be added as a consequent of the resulting disturbance of the equation of international demand.

Within the country itself, the effect of a national debt on the distribution of wealth is also undesirable. It increases the gross amount of profits at the expense of the wages-fund and real wages. The capital of such country will soon be just what it would have been if the debt had not been created, and it will demand and receive the same rate and amount of profit. As the gross product is not increased, whatever income capitalists obtain from the advances they have made to the government, is ultimately derived, through prices, from the consumers, and, in so far as laborers are consumers, from real wages. Although, therefore, the immediate effect of the payment of the national obligations is detrimental to the laboring classes, on account of the decreased production and lessened employment it temporarily causes, the ultimate effect will be beneficial, in that it will give them a larger normal share of the gross product.

Our principle also profoundly affects the controversy between the bi-metallists and the advocates of a single standard, and should, I think, settle the controversy in favor of the former. The claim of the latter that the relative value of the two precious metals depends upon the cost of production, and can not be arbitrarily fixed, as it must be, if both metals are to be used, seems to me fallacious. So much the greater part of their value is due to their use as mediums of exchange, that all nations agreeing to use them interchangeably in any fixed proportion, not too much at variance with their value for other purposes, would reduce the two metals, for the purpose of scientific discussion, to one commodity. As the utility of the two would be not only equal but identical, the effect of any relative increase in the cost of the production of either would not change their relative value, but only enhance the rentals of the mines from which the other was exploited. Thus, if the only use of wheat or of rye was to make bread, and the bread from either grain was absolutely indistinguishable from that made from the other, the relative value of the two grains could never differ. If an improvement in agriculture should enable wheat to be raised at less than its former cost, while the production of rye was unaffected, wheat would not thereby sell for less than rye, but more of it and less of rye would be grown, and lands adapted to wheat would bring higher rentals. The real utility of both gold and silver is artificial and identical, and their value in relation to each other can consequently be arbitrarily fixed, if only the agreement to do so be complete. Their value as compared with articles of natural utility is not subject, of course, to arbitrary adjustment, but their value relative to each other can be, at least, within the limit that neither shall be cheaper than its value for other utilities than that of serving as a medium of exchange.

Assuming that the ratio between the two can be fixed, the demonetization of silver amounts simply to a world-wide contraction of the currency.

The influence of price on industrial activity is not sufficiently recognized, nor can it be, while the amount of activity is supposed to increase or decrease with the amount of capital. The principle here advanced that, under our present economic organization, profit being the sole stimulus to production, industrial activity will vary with the rate of profit, within the limit of the physical sufficiency of capital to supply the fund for wages, leads us to attach a new importance to the phenomena of price.

A rise in prices, however equal and uniform it may be, transfers value from the creditor to the debtor class. This encourages production, not only because the latter are pre-eminently the class upon whom the amount of production depends, but because, in such times, the risk of giving credit being lessened, the credit system itself is extended. But a rise in prices is never equal and uniform. Any difference in the prices of different material commodities, however it may change the direction, has little or no influence upon the gross amount of production; but other commodities advancing in price more rapidly than labor, stimulates production, because thereby profits are enhanced. Any rise in the price of labor more rapid than that of material commodities, or decline in the latter more rapid than the decline in wages, has, of course, the contrary effect, and serves to limit and repress production.

There is one peculiarity of the exchangeable value of labor, to which, although it is involved in what I have said, it would perhaps have been better to have pointed more distinctly earlier in the argument. The exchangeable value of any article, however much it may vary, can never exceed its supposed utility; but productive labor has absolutely no utility of itself, it is never worth more than it will produce; consequently its value can never rise above the value or supposed value of what it can produce, less a satisfactory profit to its employer. In proportion as its value is less than this, will capitalists seek to employ it, and the sum of production be the greater and the total wages-fund increased. When any material commodity, on account of its scarcity, increases in value, the total amount of it in existence may exchange for a greater, the same, or a less amount of other things than before. When the cost of labor is enhanced on account of its scarcity, as compared with the sum total of existent material products, the total amount exchanged (i. e., employed) will *only* obtain a smaller sum total than before, because what is not employed, as it can not be reserved, is lost to its possessors for ever.

The price of labor is affected by another peculiarity. During any period of rise or of fall in general prices, labor is among the last of the commodities to be affected. Its rise or fall follows that of the material commodities it produces only after a considerable interval. It consequently happens that any period of advancing prices is also a period of great industrial activity, and a period of declining prices one of industrial stagnation. An ephemeral rise is, to be sure, of only transient advantage, and, as I have elsewhere shown, more than compensated for by the results of the ensuing decline—i. e., the sum total of the production of both periods is less than if prices had remained uniform at their normal figure. But when the advance in prices is maintained, the advantage gained by it, and the accumulation it justifies, are retained. This explains why the industrial development of the civilized world, which we are yet enjoying, was coincident in its commencement with the discovery of the mines of Mexico and Peru. And that this development has been sustained to the present time by the discovery and exploitation of the mines of the United States, Australia, and Siberia, history does not allow us to doubt, although other powerful causes, such as the advance in science and the arts, greater freedom of individual and social action, and the greater abundance and availability of fertile land, have contributed to the result.

The increase of material wealth and in the activity of exchanges, as well as the growth of population, act as a drag upon the gradual and permanent rise in general prices to which they largely owe their being. Vast as has been the increase of the world's circulating medium, and greatly as its efficiency has been increased by the development of the credit system, the activity of exchanges has increased in nearly equal proportion.

When the system of co-operation is fully organized and established it will not be so, but as long as production is carried on, on the basis of the wages system, a gradual and permanent decline in prices must entail a gradual and permanent decline in production, or at least greatly retard its increase. Such a period must be one in which the average rate of profit is smaller, and the employment of labor less, than when the general tendency of prices is to advance. Under co-operation, the inducement to produce will not so much be profit, as the desire to utilize labor; but, while employer and employé are distinct persons, the amount of production must wholly depend on the rate of profit, and anything that lowers that rate, as a gradual and permanent decline in prices would do, can not but depress industry.

The demonetization of silver, if it becomes general, will undoubtedly depress prices to somewhere about the point they reached in the middle ages, and will entail an incalculable but enormous decline in the material prosperity of the world. The adoption of that policy by England, Germany, and the United States was mainly responsible for the severity and long continuance of our last period of depression, and, if it is continued by these nations and adopted by others, we may expect our periods of industrial activity to be shorter and less gainful, and our periods of depression to be longer and more severe, than they have heretofore been; and to such degree will this result as, in all probability, to place the world in the retrogressive state in which the total production will annually decline.

Any increase of the medium of exchange, founded on the solid basis of an increase of the precious metals, or on that of a legitimate and safe extension of credit, yields benefits analogous to those derived from an inflation of the currency, without the drawback of the ensuing contraction, that must occur when it is founded on an unsubstantial basis, or confined to the limited area of a single nation. Advancing civilization demands not only an equivalent but a somewhat greater increase in the medium of exchange, and can not proceed without it, as long as labor continues to be a commodity.

The above observations on prices and the medium of circulation serve to explain the anxiety with which commercial men watch the rate of international exchange and the importation or exportation of gold. It is not because they are yet infected with the exploded fallacies of the mercantile system, but because experience has taught them that the increase of the circulating medium means a period of higher prices, greater profits, and increased industry, and that the exportation of gold is a warning to prepare for lower prices, declining profits, and industrial stagnation.

Further instances could be multiplied where theories are modified and facts explained by the recognition of the law I have attempted to enunciate and elucidate—the ramifications of the subject are endless and lead in every direction. As the purpose of this work is rather to substantiate than to apply the main principle involved, enough has been said on these points, except to call attention to the fact that the law, which I have endeavored to explain, affects social questions as powerfully as it does economic. These have, to some extent, been considered, but only when they were involved in the economic questions under review. Considering them as beyond the strict domains of our science, and as belonging to a higher one, it would have been out of place to attempt to consider them in their full bearings, and I only mention them here, that it may not be supposed I am oblivious of their relation to the subject.

CHAPTER XVIII.

CONCLUSION.

Although it will involve some repetition, a gathering together of the principal results obtained into a condensation of my argument will not be out of place.

We have first found an important variation in the definitions of capital, as given by Ricardo and Mill, and have seen that that of the former is defective; and that, while Mill has rectified the definition of Ricardo, he has adopted the latter's deductions, without perceiving that they were only applicable to capital in the limited sense in which Ricardo used the term. We have then made the deduction that over-accumulation—meaning by that term an increase of capital beyond the needs of population—is not only possible, as Mill and Ricardo both acknowledge, but of frequent and periodic occurrence in all civilized nations, and that it is so was proved by the irrefutable test of the rate of profit during times of depression, and the periodic occurrence of such times—the low rate that always obtains in such periods being a certain indication that capital is then superabundant.

We then noticed that the distinction between dead and active stock, although perceived and acknowledged by both economists, was practically ignored in their arguments.

We also noticed that the over-accumulation which is

here contended for does not at all conflict with the results obtained by Say from a consideration of the laws of supply and demand, but, on the contrary, is in full accordance with them, labor being considered as a commodity. We also detected Mill in an erroneous use of the word "market," and found that the word really refers, not to the possibility of exchanging at any price, but only to the possibility of goods exchanging for the value of the labor that will reproduce them with some profit, and that a market is good or bad in proportion as such profit is great or small.

We also ascertained that the adjustment of the ratio of capital to population, when producers are influenced in their production by the hope of gain, could only practically be obtained by a sufficient cessation from further production, and that the consequent lack of employment overbalanced to the laborers the accompanying rise in their rate of proportional wages.

In the further pursuit of the argument we were able to rightly discriminate between proportional and real wages, and to show that they varied inversely instead of together, as has heretofore been assumed. This, again, led us to valuable conclusions on the labor question, socialism, and co-operation, and enabled us to make the important deduction that a high rate of proportional wages is not, as Mill and Ricardo everywhere assume, a stimulus to population, but the reverse—the real stimulus being the rate of real wages, that varies inversely with it. And this deduction threw some further light upon the labor question, and showed that the efforts of the laborers, through their present organizations, to raise money and proportional but not real wages, are very prejudicial to their own interests.

We were then enabled to arrive at a complete and satisfactory explanation of commercial crises and the industrial stagnation which invariably follows them, a hitherto unsolved problem of the science. We were also enabled, as never before, to understand the economic nature and action of credit, and to correct several misconceptions on the subject.

Having established the fact that capital in civilized countries constantly tends to an over-increase, it of course followed that a country would very soon obtain any additional capital demanded by an increase in its population or by a change in the nature of its industries, and that such increase would be the fruit of labor that would otherwise have been wasted in idleness. This enabled us to undermine the fundamental premise of free trade, in so far as the distribution of wealth is concerned. We saw that the gain or loss to an individual nation of importing foreign goods was not to be computed from a comparison of the price at which a commodity could be imported with the price at which it could be made at home, but from a comparison of its imported cost with the cost alone of the labor which would be diverted to its manufacture. We further showed that what caused nations to manufacture instead of to cultivate the soil was, to but a slight degree, any advantage possessed over their neighbors in manufacturing itself, but was mainly the lowness of their own margin of cultivation. A further consideration of the inherent nature of agriculture and manufacture showed the latter to possess great economic advantages over the former as a national pursuit, and to such degree that, as a matter of fact, some countries, with the least natural facilities for production, had greatly the advantage over their more favored neighbors in the amount of their capitalized wealth, and were able to equal them in the value *per capita* of their annual product, notwithstanding a great difference in the respective efficiency of their labor; and we saw that this unnatural result was accomplished through the profits, that nations with a high margin of cultivation could appropriate to themselves, through a protective policy alone, and that the gain of such policy, if wisely pursued, would overbalance any loss in the efficiency of labor that resulted from its being diverted from agriculture.

A consideration of the equation of international demand, based entirely upon Mill's premises, and with some trivial exceptions upon his deductions, also showed us that the equation, in the nature of things, when commerce is unrestricted, must be against an agricultural country; and led us to the new and important principle that the gain of the manufacturing country will not express itself in its rate of manufacturing profit, but in the amount of its dead stock and the gross amount of its profits thereon. This heretofore unobserved circumstance enabled us to appreciate as never before the practical working of the equation itself, and explained the fact that manufacturing are the lending nations of the world. We then considered the distribution of wealth in a protected country, and found that, though not as beneficial to its laboring classes as could be wished, it yet worked somewhat to their advantage, especially when the policy was first adopted. We ascertained, in the course of our argument, that a manufacturing country can not protect itself against an agricultural, and only injures itself by the attempt, and that the policy of "fair trade," coming into favor in England, is illusory in its promises. We also discovered that the nations now benefited by free trade will, in the near future, be forced into competition with nations of a yet lower margin of cultivation, and, when this happens, that their industry can only be preserved, and that but partially, by they themselves adopting the policy they now denounce.

A discussion of rent elucidated the fact that there is an hitherto unnoticed difference in the effect upon prices of that portion of it due to inherent fertility and that due to propinquity to market, and that the latter does affect the comparative value and price of manufactured goods, and is at the expense of the consumer of such goods wherever consumed, and that, when such consumer is a foreigner, such portion of rental is a tribute laid by one country upon another.

A consideration of commerce, hitherto left out of the discussion, showed it to possess advantages as a national pursuit superior even to manufactures, but that it could only be protected in the form of subsidies granted to it, and we obtained suggestions as to our own national policy of the greatest value.

Finally, we found that the admitted loss to the world, in the efficiency of its labor caused by protection, was only the price that must be paid for a better final distribution of its labor and capital; and, although we were unable to determine whether the result was fully worth the price, we did find several indications that it was sufficiently so to remove the moral stigma of national selfishness from those nations who adopt the policy.

Lastly, our principle threw greatly needed light on the subjects of taxation and national indebtedness, and afforded a basis for a positive decision in favor of bimetallism.

Affecting all these questions as it does, the importance

of the principle that, in countries where law and order prevail, the tendency of capital is to outstrip population, can hardly be overestimated. It effects as great a revolution in economic ideas as any single principle ever enunciated. Whether I have established it as a leading principle of the science must be left to the reader to judge. It certainly seems to me to be in accordance with every fact of history and experience, to throw light on many intricate subjects not hitherto understood, and to have a practical bearing in the application of the science, that will remove from it the stigma of consisting mainly of inapplicable theories—an objection hitherto too well founded on fact. And, lastly, I can not but feel it to be in the line of and in full accord with all well-established economic laws, and, however inconsistent with their final conclusions, purely the logical result of the thoughts and teachings of the three great masters of political economy, Smith, Ricardo, and Mill; for which reasons I venture to hope for this treatise a more kindly reception than theories of over-accumulation have heretofore received.

THE END.